"You, the reader, may be asking, 'How may I discern and enrich the shape of my own character, caught as I am in my unreliable human mind and body?' Based on her own counseling and life experience, Helen Cepero brings some wise and valuable suggestions, enlarging on the three simple key words: *faith, hope, love.*"

Luci Shaw, author of *Breath for the Bones* and *Adventure of Ascent*

"Helen's unique ability to tell her story with such vulnerability and ask penetrating, grace-filled questions creates a safe environment for the personal work of the Spirit in one's life. Thank you for opening yet another door for a healthy and holy journey into God's presence."

Rev. Mark A. Novak, Ordered Ministry, Evangelical Covenant Church

"Helen Cepero's book—with an indirect directness—confronts, convicts and then converses the reader into the formative practices of the three theological virtues: love, faith and hope. Conversant with both classical and contemporary spiritual theology and especially the Bible, this book opens one genuinely to St. Benedict's *conversio* and the joy of newness of life."

John Weborg, professor emeritus, North Park Theological Seminary

"*Christ-Shaped Character* is more than a book. It is a conversation with a spiritual director, whom you will find a welcoming fellow traveler on the Jesus way. As you read Helen Cepero's work, you will discover her listening attentively to your own story and offering your story back to you framed by faith, hope and love. You will come away with more than principles and practical recommendations for spiritual formation. In pondering Helen's stories and perspectives, you will receive fresh insight into your own story shaped by God's love in Christ. Read carefully and enjoy the conversation."

Paul Louis Metzger, professor of Christian theology and theology of culture, Multnomah Biblical Seminary

"Transformation of our character—becoming like Jesus and changing into people of faith, hope and love—is the heart of Christianity. This sort of renovation doesn't happen automatically or magically. Helen Cepero offers biblical wisdom and practical direction for cooperating with the Holy Spirit for life change. Her gentle wisdom can help you choose life."

Adele Calhoun, author of *Spiritual Disciplines Handbook* and copastor, Redeemer Community Church

"In *Christ-Shaped Character*, Helen Cepero, an experienced spiritual director, invites us to journey together and ponder nine life-giving pathways that lead toward being more Christ-shaped. Through her own personal stories of 'aha moments' and dark valleys, Cepero creates an atmosphere of grace and transparency, offering a safe place to honestly reflect on our own inner movements, as if sitting in a welcoming direction session with her, conversing about life and God. Cepero is an insightful guide to help us deepen our love, our faith and our hope."

Klaus Issler, Talbot School of Theology, Biola University; author of *Living into the Life of Jesus*

"Biblically grounded and richly illustrated with personal stories, *Christ-Shaped Character* offers a solid and appealing spirituality. Helen Cepero provides practical and insightful ways of living a vibrant life of faith, centered on a warm and trusting relationship with a God who loves us unconditionally. She shares her story of finding God in the holy ground of ordinary experience with such sensitivity and joy that readers will be inspired to be more attentive to the many ways—sometimes surprising—that God shows up to lovingly support us in life. I recommend her book enthusiastically."

Wilkie Au, author of *The Enduring Heart: Spirituality for the Long Haul*

"It has been said, 'To pay attention is the beginning of faith, hope and love.' Through the artful telling of her own story, Helen has opened a way for us to pay deep attention to our own lives and to find God at every turn. Here is the voice of a pastor's pastor and one who is deeply skilled in the discernment arts of spiritual direction. Pay attention and be blessed."

Rev. Dr. David Kersten, dean, North Park Theological Seminary

"Helen Cepero just has this evocative way of driving home her main points via compelling stories of faith, hope and love. The book is at once both arresting and revealing! Truly a joy to read!"

Wil Hernandez, founder and president of CenterQuest and author of a trilogy on Henri Nouwen

"Cepero hasn't just written about love, faith and hope, but about actually doing it. She paints a picture of what it looks like to do it and then gives you practices to get you on your way."

Jan Johnson, author of *Abundant Simplicity* and *Spiritual Disciplines Companion*

CHRIST-SHAPED CHARACTER

CHOOSING LOVE, FAITH AND HOPE

HELEN CEPERO

IVP Books

An imprint of InterVarsity Press
Downers Grove, Illinois

InterVarsity Press
P.O. Box 1400, Downers Grove, IL 60515-1426
World Wide Web: www.ivpress.com
Email: email@ivpress.com

InterVarsity Press® is the book-publishing division of InterVarsity Christian Fellowship/USA®, a movement of students and faculty active on campus at hundreds of universities, colleges and schools of nursing in the United States of America, and a member movement of the International Fellowship of Evangelical Students. For information about local and regional activities, write Public Relations Dept., InterVarsity Christian Fellowship/USA, 6400 Schroeder Rd., P.O. Box 7895, Madison, WI 53707-7895, or visit the IVCF website at www.intervarsity.org.

Scripture quotations, unless otherwise noted, are from the New Revised Standard Version of the Bible, copyright 1989 by the Division of Christian Education of the National Council of the Churches of Christ in the USA. Used by permission. All rights reserved.

Parts of chapter 5 appeared in the February 2012 volume of Covenant Companion *as "Embracing Vulnerability."*

Parts of chapter 6 appeared in the December 2004 volume of Covenant Companion *as "The Dead are Still with Us."*

While all stories in this book are true, some names and identifying information in this book have been changed to protect the privacy of the individuals involved.

Cover design: Cindy Kiple
Interior design: Beth Hagenberg
Images: boardwalk through dunes: © drnadig/iStockphoto; jungle boardwalk: © andrearoad/
  iStockphoto; farm road: © konradlew/iStockphoto; forest path: © Nikada/iStockphoto; forest
  path: © borchee/iStockphoto; boardwalk in dunes: © PPAMPicture/iStockphoto; pathway to
  beach: © Turnervisual/iStockphoto; dirt path in the woods: © tiburonstudios/iStockphoto;
  winding pathway: © InCommunicado/iStockphoto

ISBN 978-0-8308-3582-9 (print)
ISBN 978-0-8308-9592-2 (digital)

Printed in the United States of America ∞

Library of Congress Cataloging-in-Publication Data
A catalog record for this book is available from the Library of Congress.

P	19	18	17	16	15	14	13	12	11	10	9	8	7	6	5	4	3	2	1

Y	30	29	28	27	26	25	24	23	22	21	20	19	18	17	16	15	14

To my husband Max Lopez-Cepero for
his unfailing loyalty and support

And now faith, hope, and love abide, these three;
and the greatest of these is love.

1 CORINTHIANS 13:13

Contents

Introduction

*I*t is about 2:00 a.m. when my feet hit the soft grass under the bedroom window of my ranch-style home. I walk down the silent street of the small Wisconsin village until I am able to go "cross-lots" through backyards with their still swing sets and empty lawn chairs. Then I follow my own path under the goalposts of the high school football field until I am standing before the door of a church. Sunday mornings I arrive at this same church in my "good clothes." But tonight as I open the heavy oak door with its brass handle, I am a thirteen-year-old barefoot supplicant in cutoffs and a T-shirt. I walk down the aisle and sit in a pew, finding in the darkness what I long for—a transcendent Presence that I somehow misplaced during the daylight hours of home and high school and church.

In the night's shadow, the space is both empty and full to me. It is empty of all the whispering judgments of this small community, but full of a sense of belonging that has held me since my birth. It is empty of the fearful sermons about a God who seems always on the edge of anger. But it is full of the God of the Bible and all its colorful, storied characters. Melodies of "blessed assurance" and "leaning on the everlasting arms" echo through the ceiling rafters high above me. But there is something else too. I hear whispers in the "sounds of silence," an utterly new sound to me but one referenced in my favorite radio song. Though only moonlight visibly floods this austere sanctuary, in those prophetic whispers the presence of Christ's Spirit is tangible.

That Presence surrounds me and fills me. In the spaciousness of what is and what is not, I am able to rest. The Spirit of God is welcoming of all that is and has been and will be, all that threatens to overwhelm my insecure teenage self. Here I experience God's love, and even God's hopeful liking of who I am.

Though my time in the church is short, I stay long enough to sense that this Something, and this Someone, is missing from my daytime world and yet a part of it as well. For a few blessed moments I even feel the peace that passes understanding (Philippians 4:7) holding my mind and heart. Then I retrace my steps, walking back across the football field and the backyards and down Main Street, until I noiselessly crawl back through my bedroom window and finish my night's sleep.

As a teenager I felt that such experiences were utterly unique to me. My own family, even my closest friend, was unaware of my nightly sojourns during that summer. I never spoke about them with anyone, convinced that people might think me a little off my spiritual rocker. But now I've heard and read enough to know that I was not and am not alone in my experience. This sense of spiritual awareness, even mystical presence, is extraordinary in one way but also meant to be an ordinary part of everyday life. It is as if the Cloud of Unknowing[1] is thinned at those moments and we see this oneness with God in our life, the really real of all that is.

What I know now from my own life and listening to the lives of others is that there is always a path that goes "cross-lots" through our lives. There is always a doorway. This book is about finding those doorways into life with God, and about exploring what we find when we open those doors. It will help you see how values and virtues grow out of our experiences, and it describes practices that encourage us to be with. I've seen that when I reflect on my own life experiences, when I am alert to God's presence and alive to Christ's love, I grow as a Christ-follower and as a human being living in God's world. This book is an invitation for you not to follow me but to follow Jesus into the stories of your own life. You, too, will need to wake up and be willing to walk cross-lots through your own life, to open the door and enter in.

This journey follows along the way of love, faith and hope. The apostle Paul wrote to the Corinthians, "Now faith, hope, and love abide, these three; and the greatest of these is love" (1 Corinthians 13:13). He calls love "a more excellent way" to begin our life in Christ because he knows that without a firm grounding in love, faith will falter and hope will be lost. So we will follow the journey through, beginning with three ways of love, then three ways of continuing in faith, and lastly three ways of living in hope. I plot out these nine pathways of living in Christ through love, faith and hope in reference to stories from my life; I hope they will resonate with you as we travel together.

You will want to put a few helpful things in your backpack as you begin this trek with me. One of them is a journal, whether it be pen and paper or a computer file, or maybe a sketch pad if your responses are more visual than worded. Each chapter will have a stopping place with a suggestion for reflection on your own life. You might pause there, or you might continue on instead in the chapter, returning later for a closer look at how what you read might speak into your life. If you have a tendency to get lost, as I do, this stopping place will help you to locate the "You are here" spot on your life's path.

You might also want to pack a bit of time to experiment with prayer. Each chapter suggests a practice designed to help you grow into deeper life in love, faith and hope in Christ. Remember that prayer practices can be awkward or even difficult when you first try them. With a new tool or musical instrument, it often takes time to get the knack of using it to repair furniture or play a melody. So it is with prayer. I encourage you, then, to keep at it for a number of days, so that a prayer melody can be discerned or this prayer tool find its usefulness. My second suggestion is equally important. Playing an instrument long enough to discern a melody or finding just the right tool to accomplish a job can be fun and surprisingly satisfying. Allow space for this feeling of satisfaction and enjoyment to be part of your growing life in Christ.

Most important of all, you will need to bring your own story. Each chapter of the book begins with a story from my life, as does this introduction. Sometimes I wrote the story first and then saw the way it illustrated an underlying value or an enduring purpose. Other times I was aware of wanting to write about an aspect of love or faith or hope, and I remembered a story that somehow reflected that particular virtue. My goal is not that you would simply enjoy my stories, although that would give me pleasure; nor do I primarily want to teach you insights into life, although if that happens I will be delighted. A more fundamental goal as I tell my stories is that they help you remember your own stories—the stories of love, stories of faith, stories of hope in your life—and that my insights, or the insights of others, give you insight into how you might live each day more fully alive in Christ. The listening suggestions at the end of each chapter are written to personally engage you in remembering and naming your own stories of love, faith and hope.

Living fully alive in Christ is about claiming an identity. An identity is formed not just by doctrine or prescription, or even insight and stated values, but by stories that we live and those that are told to us. Daniel Taylor writes: "We tell stories because our lives present themselves to us in story form: setting, characters, plot. . . . We tell and listen to stories obsessively because nothing else so compelling organizes the disparate bits of our lives. . . . We don't simply hear stories, we live within them."[2] Certainly we see and share this in the Bible's stories of love and faith and hope. But if we are to live in Christ, fully alive, it must be articulated in our story as well.

Understanding and living our stories of love, faith and hope is a calling for us personally and in our communities as well. The psalmist invites us to this same storied reflection when he instructs, "Let the redeemed of the LORD tell their story." Then he tells story after story of God's redemption through desert, darkness, rebellion and shipwreck, finally ending with this call: "Let the one who is wise heed these things and ponder the loving deeds of the LORD" (Psalm 107:2, 43 NIV).

PART ONE

Choosing Love

1

Choosing Life

Living as God's Beloved

*T*he percussionist in the back of the Beginners' Band is only rarely, and then almost by chance, hitting the snare drum on the beat. But nobody could miss in his wide, toothy smile the pure joy he finds in hearing the drumsticks make that reverberating racket. The band members in front of him don't seem to notice or care about the lack of any consistent beat; they concentrate on their own instruments. The woodwind players are seriously intent on getting recognizable notes out of their squeaking clarinets, flutes and saxophones while trying to hear a melody somewhere nearby. The trumpets play loudly, though only occasionally producing sounds that seem connected to the notes on their music stands. The frustrated band director stands in front of them all, wearing the look of one who must endure to the end what cannot turn out good or even passable. He audibly hums the theme while directing large, each and every beat, but no one in the Beginners' Band is paying much attention to him. And neither is the raptly attentive audience of parents.

I am sitting near the front, my gaze fixed on a ten-year-old girl in the obligatory white blouse and black skirt, her face red with the effort of playing the trumpet. Awkwardly trying to hold the trumpet up, she enters on the wrong beat with a honking sound where there is a clearly meant to be a rest. But her face is a study in concentration as she tries to count out each measure and sends an occasional passing glance toward the conductor on the podium. At home this same girl can seem irritatingly careless about living out her life's details. But now I see a glimpse of the poised, knowing woman she may become, and I am mesmerized. I've fallen in love yet again with my own child.

Next to me, another mother's attention is similarly focused on just one student, though with all the students sitting so close together it is difficult to see which child is holding her gaze. But as the band finally finishes its first number, her excitement spills over to my seat, and she turns to me with tears in her eyes. "That's my son Darrin in the back, playing the snare drum. Isn't he just great?" I see that she too has fallen in love with her own child. She is certain that her son stands out clearly, not just loudly, as outstanding to me as he is to her. My eyes fill with tears as well as I whisper, pointing out the trumpeter in the fourth chair of the second row: "And that's my daughter, Leana— just look at her." The other mother hands me a tissue, and we both wipe our eyes, eagerly awaiting the next raucous number the band will play.

I admit it. I have always loved the Beginners' Band concerts. I love the heroic effort of all these beginners trying to play something together—the serious intention of it all. I love the peek it gives us all into what might be—the possibility of actually making harmonious music together. It is both the fruit of (at least some) practice and the promise of what might yet be. I also admit that no one except parents usually hears the prescient musical possibilities at these concerts. But we mothers do not miss the recurring theme of a beginning attentiveness to the music that is both within our own child and beyond her or him. We know just taking up an instrument and joining a band is a commitment to the possibility of creating music, alone and together, that is a gift to the audience as well as themselves.

In the matter of Christ-shaped character, we are much like the students in the Beginners' Band. We can see the music, but actually knowing when to play and when to rest, landing on the beat and doing this alongside others, can seem daunting. Whether we come with a longing to hear music above the needy cacophony of our lives or in the numbing absence of any meaningful sounds, we have joined the band of faith to try to hear the tune and find the rhythm of our lives. Some of us work so hard at our character that we miss the joy in the music; others deal with the task of living in Christ so casually that we never come to understand the music at all. Perhaps lurking behind both our hard work and our inattention are questions we fear to voice: What if all the others manage to get in tune readily but I stay stuck in this place of discord? What if others can find rhythm and I'm left behind?

Most of us have the idea that in this drama of the life of faith, God plays the role of the surly and impatient or stoic and resigned band director who is frustrated at his students' inability to make proper music or even find the beat. Sometimes we do not even begin for fear we will play a wrong note and then be silenced or made to play alone in front of everybody else. In the end it is only the urgent need to hear some overarching melody in our life, or some rhythmic beat, that keeps us from putting our instrument down on the chair and walking away from the band altogether.

But what if God is really more like the parents who sit in the audience and listen with rapt attention, their eyes focused on their own son or daughter? This One is watching with tears in those holy eyes, seeing not just the careful concentration but the posture and poise and possibility of living into another way of being. Just showing up with our intention to play music with God is a commitment to the melody that is already within us. Even the beginning of this sound is a gift not just to us but to the surrounding world. Finding the holy courage to enter into life with God in community is the way home to our true selves, as well as to God; it is a way of attending to the sound that is within us and beyond.

Trying to please God, rather than live as God's beloved in Christ, leaves us dependent on our own effort, our own striving toward our idealized picture of ourselves. We are comfortable with our holy to-do lists of what we believe will make us acceptable to ourselves, to others and to God. The truth is that much in the Christian culture supports these vigorous attempts to seek significance or security on our own or to earn God's favor. But these efforts at self-realization are inevitably motivated not by love or a sense of identity in Christ but by guilt or even fear. Ultimately they will fail.

In *Invitation to Love*, Thomas Keating tells the story of his own performing self. After taking vows and joining the Trappist order, Keating resolved to be the best monk he could possibly be. When his community was fasting, Keating fasted longer and with more asceticism than anyone else. When the brothers went to prayer, Keating remained in the chapel long after the others had gone to bed. But when he went to his superior expecting to be lauded for his dedication, he was disappointed to find that the abbot was not impressed. Instead he was disturbed that

Keating, for all his effort, had entirely missed the point. His coming into the monastic community was not about going deeper into his own striving. It was instead an invitation to trust in God's love for him, not his ascetic expectations for himself.[1]

What gives the development of Christ-shaped life meaning and purpose is God's look of love toward each of us. This is not first of all a place of doing but a place of *being*, where we listen and receive God's love for us. It is in this gaze of God through Jesus Christ that we realize nothing we do will make God love us more; nothing we do will make God love us less. When we are rooted in this place of transforming love, we don't push toward a goal that is beyond our circumstances or abilities; rather, our actions move toward the hope that is already in us.

Eight months after listening to my daughter and the rest of the Beginners' Band attempt to play publicly together for the first time, I return to hear the same band, dressed in similar white-and-black attire. Now they are no longer the Beginners' Band but officially the Intermediate Jazz Band. There is Darrin again on the snare drums, with the same wide, toothy grin, only this time there are braces on those teeth. And now this young percussionist is able to follow the beat while paying careful attention to the band director, offering rhythmic continuity to the whole band. My own daughter, taller now and holding her trumpet at the ready, watches the director, plays and then counts out the rests in between the notes so that she can enter the music when her next turn comes. But then something surprises the audience and brings us to our feet.

After they play their first number together, the band members step out from the band one at a time and walk up to the microphone to solo. Still following the chords and the beat of the song, these young musicians are able to improvise a unique movement and melody while the band plays the rhythmic theme behind them. Even when mistakes are made, they are woven into the larger jazz melody. Each soloist soars to find new notes connected to the musical chords and then returns to the original tune as the rest of the band joins in. We clap loud and long for each courageous student who comes forward to solo, including Darrin and Leana.

Perhaps living fully alive in Christ, like playing in the jazz band, is not about following the rules and doing everything right but is about learning to soar. It is about taking a risk, finding your own jazz melody and not being afraid to step up to the microphone and let yourself be heard. Maybe this is what the apostle Paul meant when he invited us to "work out [our] own salvation with fear and trembling" (Philippians 2:12). When we are living out of our true identity as God's beloved, we can improvise out of who we are in Christ. And we do this not only as soloists but with others, as we listen and receive a theme, play it out in our lives, and hand it back to others and God.

Finding this melody is the way into the arms of a God who loves us and yearns to hear our unique melody, the voice of our imagination, the depth of our silent pauses, the surge of our feelings or our tentative insights. We are created to find in the very act of living every day a way to play that loves us into expressing our transcendent self. When we step up to the microphone and risk our own jazz melody, all God's angels rise up, spread their angelic wings and clap loud and long.

Taking a Closer Look: Caring for Our Inner Critic

Many of us have an inner critic that seeks to be the motivating force in our lives. Sometimes we hear its voice when we get defensive and say, "It isn't fair," or "I'm right," or "It wasn't my fault." When we are stressed, that inner critic can be a bully, threatening and blaming others. At other times the inner critic blames or even condemns us, saying, "It's all my fault," or "I'm no good," or "I know I can't do this," and we nod in resigned agreement. Whether we blame ourselves or defend ourselves or ridicule others, the inner critic will always seek to motivate our actions out of fear or guilt or anger or pride. While the inner critic claims to be our friend, to be on our side, its words are never words of love. If you follow its advice, you will find your life self-focused: your character will be not be formed in love but in effort and striving. It will inevitably lead you toward the performing self and away from God's love. It will be up to you to succeed or fail on your own.

Perhaps as you've listened to yourself you can easily identify your inner critic, the one who accuses rather than loves. For some the critic even has the name of a parent or teacher or friend that hurt or betrayed you; others of us might not identify the inner critic so quickly. But if you think back to a time recently or in your childhood when you felt attacked or as if you failed in some way, you will hear the rant of the inner critic.

Take your journal and simply listen to the inner critic without judgment; just record what you hear as a journalist might quote a particular source. If it helps to give the voice a specific name, you can do that as well. Now take a look at the past twenty-four hours: Which of your actions were motivated from the voice of that inner critic? Which of your actions were motivated by a response to God's love? Each time our desire and actions are formed out of the inner critic's voice, we are moving away from God and his love. Every time we are responding to God's love, we are moving closer to our true identity as God's beloved.

Now ask yourself: *What is the longing I hear underneath the critic's negative message?*

The truth is that the inner critic is the most unloved part of us—and it is the very heart of where God most longs to live. The psalmist describes this with the Hebrew word *hesed*: the love that cannot stop loving, even during times when we feel most afflicted, as did the writer of Lamentations: "The steadfast love [*hesed*] of the LORD never ceases, his mercies never come to an end; they are new every morning; great is your faithfulness. 'The LORD is my portion,' says my soul, 'therefore I will hope in him'" (Lamentations 3:22-24). The deeper desire of the inner critic is one with God's own desire to accept and love, to choose and free, to offer a sense of belonging and home. What might it be like to allow even the inner critic to live as God's beloved? Jesus said, "I came that they may have life, and have it abundantly" (John 10:10). This was not just for part of us, but a love offered to all of who we are, even the parts of us that we find unlovable.

Prayer Practice: Breath Prayer

The spiritual practices that will call us forward into living as God's beloved are practices that teach us to loosen our tight grasp on own abilities or talents, our securities and status. One of those practices is the breath prayer. Because the act of breathing itself is unconscious, it requires us only to pay attention to life at its most basic and elemental. I remember childhood contests to see who could "hold their breath" the longest, but we could not force ourselves to stop breathing without passing out, fainting and then breathing again. To pray the breath prayer, we pay attention to our breath as I did as a child, not to "hold our breath" but to be attentive to the breath and rest in the nearness of God's Spirit.

Breath is the first gift of life for each of us when we leave our mother's womb. And it was from the very beginning of life itself. When our Maker and Creator formed the first person out of the dust of the earth, God "breathed into his nostrils the breath of life; and the man became a living being" (Genesis 2:7). And it was also the first gift that Jesus gave his disciples after the resurrection. When the disciples had gathered fearfully behind a locked door, "Jesus came and stood among them and said, 'Peace be with you. . . . As the Father has sent me, so I send you.' When he had said this, he breathed on them and said to them, 'Receive the Holy Spirit'" (John 20:19-22). Both the gift of life and the gift of the Spirit within come not out of our effort but as unconscious actions that ground all of our lives. Perhaps that is why the gift of breath comes with the gift of Christ's peace.

Remembering that Christ is within you, his Spirit as near as your breath, begin by repeating any name of God that expresses your love, your relationship with God. As you inhale, breathe in that name of God for a minute or two. Now remember a deep desire of your heart, perhaps that desire that is underneath your inner critic. When you exhale, offer up the desire of your heart, keeping it simple and expressed in a few words. It is the simplicity of the prayer that allows it to be prayed over and over again throughout your day. Some simple examples of this prayer:

- breathe in "Shepherd," breathe out "bring home your child"
- breathe in "Abba," breathe out "I belong to you"
- breathe in "Lord," breathe out "here I am"
- breathe in "Jesus," breathe out "have mercy on me"[2]

Prayer teacher Richard Foster describes this as a prayer that is "discovered rather than created."[3] Another way of discovering this prayer is to say your own name aloud followed by the question Jesus asks so frequently: "What do you want?" Perhaps a single word comes to mind, "faith" or "trust" or "strength," or just a short phrase, "live in freedom" or "trust your grace."

Sometimes it takes a bit of time to really name our core desire, what we want most deeply; at other times we know immediately.

The breath prayer is meant to be prayed during times set aside for prayer, and it is meant to be remembered in the middle of one's daily activities. Each breath is meant to be a reminder of the constant presence of God. It can be the prayer that takes you to sleep and awakens you in the morning. It is simple enough to retrieve during times of pain or anxiety, suffering or grief. It can sit on the surface of your awareness or held in the depth of your heart. When it lives with us at this existential level, Foster writes that "sometimes—we reach a point beyond this prayer where we are stilled within and without. Christ is before us; Christ is behind us; Christ surrounds us and is through us. This is a point where we let go of our labor [to] simply be with God."[4]

Choosing Love

When the apostle Paul writes to the church in Ephesus, he prays that Christ might "dwell in [their] hearts" and that their lives would be "rooted and grounded" in love (Ephesians 3:17). For a beginning church, this was the point of beginning—in the love of Christ. Throughout the letters of Paul, "in Christ" becomes a place of identity, a place of transformation in love, a place of coming home to God. Living in Christ is a home, a way of being where we lose none of our uniqueness but instead discover a new life in the midst of the very center of who we are and where we live:

• dead to sin, alive to God in Christ: Romans 6:11

• free from condemnation in Christ: Romans 8:1

• members of one community in Christ: Romans 12:5

• made holy in Christ: 1 Corinthians 1:2

- shown God's grace in Christ: 1 Corinthians 1:4
- destined for resurrection in Christ: 1 Corinthians 15:22
- part of God's new creation in Christ: 2 Corinthians 5:17
- reconciled and set right with God in Christ: Galatians 2:16
- children of God in Christ: Galatians 3:26
- created for good works in Christ: Ephesians 2:10

This place of belonging with God is built on a foundation of love, the gift of faith and possibility of hope. But without a beginning in love, the faith and hope lose their meaning and their purpose. The foundation of the house of belonging is the sturdy love of Jesus Christ. Without this foundation of love, our home in Christ may even look impressive, but it will not withstand the earthquakes and hurricanes that will inevitably occur in the course of our life.

The psalmist writes of a longing to be in God's dwelling place, claiming that even one day in God's house is better than a thousand days elsewhere, and that a doorkeeper there has a more favored place that those who are comfortable dwelling in other tents (Psalm 84). But Jesus invites us to literally make a home *in him*, as he makes his home in us (John 15:4). We are to be the dwelling place of Christ. "By making his home in us he allows us to make our home in him. By entering into the intimacy of our innermost self he offers us the opportunity to enter into his own intimacy with God. By choosing us as his preferred dwelling place he invites us to choose him as our preferred dwelling place."[5]

While living in Northern California near the San Andreas Fault line, my husband and I retrofitted our home to make it safer amid the shaking rumble of earthquakes. I remember my disappointment at having to spend money on improvements that were hidden, rather than more impressive changes such as interior decoration or exterior painting. But that steel reinforcement under our home was what made the house able to withstand the strong impact of a substantial earthquake without collapsing.

In a similar way, the love of God retrofits us interiorly, making us less fearful and more able to be fully alive in Christ. God's love reminds us of our creation in the image of God and restores that image in us. This beginning in love is built by God and not us. Begun in our creation in God's image, it is continued as God in Jesus Christ makes a dwelling place among us and we are called back into our own humanity by redeeming love.

I might be tempted to spend my personal capital doing exterior work on my life to build my reputation or decorating to fit the latest spiritual fashion. I can find myself frustrated that God is less interested in whether I follow the rules than in whether I'm willing to allow Jesus to enter and renew me. But our self-worth isn't found in what we do but in our willingness to be all that we are in Christ. It is love's gift.

God invites us to make ourselves at home in his love, accepting our status as God's beloved. There is a sense of creativity and joy that can come to us when we know we are worthy in God's eyes and we are safe in God's presence. Perhaps in this place we can let go of the self-consciousness of comparing ourselves or rating our performance—which are merely symptoms of feeling unworthy. Perhaps we can simply explore what it means to live in the house of God—to live in Christ. Here we may be able to let down our outer facade and show our true face. Without this beginning in God's love and our consent to be loved, our attempts in Christ will just be an outer facade, always at risk of crumbling in the face of life's adversities.

Still, we can live in this home, this life in Christ—or not. In his reflection on Rembrandt's painting *The Return of the Prodigal*, Henri Nouwen captures all the drama of this story and the poignancy of human freedom to choose the house of love in God. Meditating on the leaving of the younger son in Jesus' parable, he writes not merely of the young man in the story but of himself as well:

> Here is the mystery of my life unveiled. I am loved so much that I am left free to leave home. The blessing is there from the beginning. I have left it and keep on leaving it. But the Father is always looking for me with outstretched arms to receive me back and whisper again in my ear: "You are my Beloved; on you my favor rests."[6]

The elder son in Jesus' story struggles even more with receiving the love of the father, though he has never left home but stayed to tend his father's fields. What Nouwen hears in the words of the elder son is a home built not on the father's love that says, "Everything I have is yours," but on a foundation of resentment. The father's joy itself can be a source of resentment when the son is filled with inner complaints and self-rejection. "The father's embrace, full of light, is God's house. All the music and dancing is there. The elder son stands outside the circle of this love, refusing to enter. The light on his face makes it clear that he, too, is called to the light, but he cannot be forced."[7]

Without trusting in God's love it is not possible to enter into God's house. "Trust is that deep inner conviction that the Father wants me home."[8] The elder son compares himself with the younger son and feels unappreciated. It seems to be our fallen human nature to take our measure against those around us. Yet in Christ there are no comparisons, only the invitation to be the Beloved. There is simply God's desire to be with me and with you. In the face of the world's darkness and our own limitations,

trusting in God's goodness and love can seem naive and too
simple. Yet choosing the love and the light that it brings is the
first real practice of living in Christ.

> This is the real discipline: It requires choosing for the light
> even when there is much darkness to frighten me, choosing
> for life even when the forces of death are so visible, and
> choosing for truth even when I am surrounded by lies. . . .
> From God's perspective, one hidden act of repentance, one
> little gesture of selfless love, one moment of true for-
> giveness is all that is needed to bring God from his throne
> to run to his retuning son and to fill the heavens with
> sounds of joy.[9]

If we trust in the love beyond all loving, the gift of faith beyond
all trusting and the blessing of hope beyond hope, then we will
find ourselves living in the "household of God whose love is
stronger than death and who empowers us to be in the world
while already belonging to the kingdom of joy. . . . The great
conversion called for by Jesus is to move from belonging to the
world to belonging to God."[10]

Living in the love of Christ, as a child in the household of
God, is the foundation of all that follows in the Christian life. If
this foundation in love and safety is not there, all of the other
attachments to living in Christ are futile. When troubles overwhelm our hearts and lives, we return to the safety of this foundation of belonging in God's house of love.

The apostle Paul writes that our beginning in love is meant to
be lived through a life in Christ that bears the marks of our place
of belonging. "For you did not receive a spirit of slavery to fall
back into fear, but you have received a spirit of adoption. . . . It
is that very Spirit bearing witness with our spirit that we are
children of God, and if children, then heirs, heirs of God and

joint heirs with Christ" (Romans 8:15-17). As heirs of God, we are called to bear the marks of our inheritance. For as we receive Christ, we are to live the Christ we receive, continuing in the path of love, faith and hope.

Living in Love as God's Beloved

Listening to my life story. As you read about the Beginners' Band, are you reminded of something that mirrors God's love in your own experience? Take a few minutes to remember the details of this experience and the feelings it caused in you then. What does remembering this make you feel now?

Listening to the biblical story. In John 14:18-23 Jesus tells his disciples that he will not leave them "orphaned" and then promises that the Father and Jesus will make their home in us. What does that mean to you? How is Jesus the home-builder in your own life?

Listening to love's continuing story. How might caring for your own inner critic make you more loving and less judgmental of others?

Further Reading

Benner, David G. *Surrender to Love: Discovering the Heart of Christian Spirituality*. Downers Grove, IL: InterVarsity Press, 2003.

Nouwen, Henri J. M. *The Return of the Prodigal Son: The Story of Homecoming*. New York: Continuum, 1999.

2

Compassionate Hospitality

Receiving the Other

When I began as a volunteer at the Center for AIDS Services, I knew little about it except that it had been started by Mother Teresa's community on a visit to Oakland, California—a part of her North American mission to care for the dying. This was several years before retroviral medications were available; a diagnosis of full-blown AIDS meant you could measure your life in days and weeks instead of years. I was assigned to the kitchen, putting food on plates for the guests eating lunch at the center. Having just come through a season of conflict as an associate pastor, I was content with this simple task and glad to spend the day away from other concerns.

After I had volunteered for a few weeks, Sister Jacinta, the center's director, looked at me curiously and asked, "Why are you staying in the kitchen?" At her urging, I began to not just serve the meal but enjoy it with the clients at the center, talking and eating and laughing with and listening to those gathered around the table.

At first I felt awkward sitting at the lunch table at the Center for AIDS services. After all, I was well, healthy, while all the people at the Center were HIV positive or had AIDS. I was straight, while many of the people at the center were gay. I was white, while many of the people at the center were members of minority groups and poor. The communities of gay people in the Bay Area were and are remarkable at caring for their own. But these men and women had mostly been rejected by their communities because they were transgendered or from ethnic-minority communities and both gay and sick, sometimes homeless.

Here I was the other. But the community also felt other to me. It wasn't long before I realized that the awkwardness belonged to me; it was not shared by the community of people there. They simply made a place for me at the table. We ate together and told our stories. I was only there once a week, but every Thursday I was both welcomed and remembered at the table.

Sister Jacinta had attended more wakes and funeral masses and memorial services than she could number. But she never forgot anyone she met, and she carried their stories within her. Even though there was grief and loss, Sister Jacinta's stories kept the dead alive and remembered. And these people within and around her were her joy. I'm sure she felt sadness, but what I remember about her is the way she celebrated the life of everyone around her, those who had died and those still living—including me. As director of the center, she trained her mostly volunteer staff by telling these stories. As I listened, I remembered reading about the desert mothers and fathers who instructed their followers with stories and aphorisms.

Sister Jacinta was an *amma*, a desert mother instructing her disciples. Her desert was not a landscape of sand and rock but a landscape of people and the wilderness of the AIDS epidemic. Hers was a radical hospitality that reached out to anyone who came across her path, including me. Sometimes she would take the train from the East Bay to San Francisco. There she found a place to sit on the steps of the Civic Center with a sandwich cut in half, waiting to see who would sit beside her. Whoever took that sandwich half became her honored companion for the afternoon, and she their listening friend.

The clients at the Center for AIDS Services offered to me just what Sister Jacinta offered to the person who sat next to her on the steps of the Civic Center. They cut their sandwiches in half and gave me a share, and I had a place at their table—the center's guests were my hosts. I knew I belonged one day during a rummage sale when a transgendered woman and I ended up bickering over the same skirt. Finally she threw up her hands and gave it to me. "You want it that bad, girl, you take it home," she said.

As I returned each week, I recognized that I experienced at the center a truer sense of belonging than I found in my own faith community. These men and women knew how to receive one another without judgment. The sick, sometimes dying community of outsiders at the Center knew about welcoming; they understood hospitality. They knew about celebrating one another's stories even when that story was one of illness and death.

What I wanted was a break from my own conflicted community. What I found was a doorway into welcome and sharing in this richer life lived among those who were poor—in health, in finances, in family. What I found was a place at the table. An encounter with the "the other" in Scripture is also surprisingly often a place of meeting God's Spirit, the presence of the Holy.

In Genesis 18, Abraham is waiting at his tent door when three strangers come walking toward him. In the ancient world, strangers were foreigners often considered dangerous. But Abraham rushes out to greet these strangers, brings them into his encampment, gives them the best that he has for travelers— water and shade—instructs his wife to bake fresh bread, and slaughters a choice, tender calf to be served to these guests. As the conversation unfolds, it is clear that the Lord himself is greeting Abraham with a seemingly impossible blessing of a child. No wonder Sarah, Abraham's wife, laughs. "The LORD said to Abraham, 'Why did Sarah laugh, and say, "Shall I indeed bear a child, now that I am old?" Is anything too wonderful for the LORD? At the set time I will return to you, in due season, and Sarah shall have a son'" (Genesis 18:13-14). Because Abraham made a place for these others, the blessing of a son and a nation followed his line.

Many years later, Abraham's grandson encounters a stranger when he is alone and terrified. Jacob is haunted by the prospect of meeting his brother Esau, whom he seriously wronged twenty years earlier. Suddenly a man appears and wrestles with him through the night. "When the man saw that he did not prevail against Jacob, he struck him on the hip socket; and Jacob's hip was put out of joint as he wrestled with him." But though the man pleads to be let go, Jacob refuses unless the stranger will bless him. "Then the man said, 'You shall no longer be called Jacob, but Israel, for you have striven with God and with humans, and have prevailed.'" Jacob asks the stranger for his name, but instead the stranger blesses him. And Jacob called that place Peniel, "for I have seen God face to face, and yet my life is preserved" (Genesis 32:25-30). Soon thereafter, when Esau embraces him with love instead of hatred, Jacob says, "Truly to see your face is like seeing the face of God" (Genesis 33:10). Perhaps it was the stranger, the other, who prepared Jacob to embrace his brother in love instead of fear.

Throughout the Gospels, the most common accusation laid on Jesus is the way he seems to enjoy the company of those considered other in Jewish society—tax collectors and "sinners." He befriends the Samaritan woman, takes pity on the hemorrhaging woman, invites himself to dinner at the home of Zacchaeus and allows a prostitute to anoint his feet with oil. Jesus breaks all of the holiness codes that carefully designate who is in and who is out, who is right and who is wrong. Insisting that holiness can appear in those considered other because of blindness or illness or even demon possession as easily (and perhaps more easily) as in the priests in the temple, Jesus with his radical hospitality infuriates the rule keepers of the Jewish community.

In Luke's Gospel there are two times when wealthy, entitled young men ask what they must do to inherit eternal life. Perhaps we, with our own bias of consumerism, remember when Jesus told the wealthy young man to sell all that he owned and follow Jesus. But Jesus' own community was probably most shocked by the other incident of a lawyer who confronted Jesus. The lawyer knows the heart of Jewish law and practice: "You shall love the Lord your God with all your heart, and with all your soul, and with all your strength, and with all your mind; and your neighbor as yourself" (Luke 10:27). But he asks the question: "Who is my neighbor?"

Jesus tells a story where a priest and a Levite pass by someone who has been assaulted, robbed and left for dead along the roadside. A despised Samaritan is the hero of the story, because he not only rescues the stranger but provides for the injured man's continuing care. The wealthy lawyer is instructed to follow the Samaritan's example of compassion and care of the stranger in need.

Every aspect of this story ignored rules of holiness and tribal loyalties to identify the neighbor as the person in need, regardless of whether he or she is part of one's community. And the example of a neighbor offering love is the person most despised in the Jewish community. But this is the person whom the lawyer is told to emulate if he wants to love his neighbor—if he wants to fulfill the law.

After the resurrection it is Jesus who is the unrecognized one, the other who turns the disciples' sad disappointment into joy. Three days after the crucifixion of Jesus, two disciples are walking home to Emmaus and a stranger joins them on their journey. The other traveler asks them why they are so sad, and they pour out their hearts to him. Instead of telling him to mind his own business, they tell the story of Jesus' execution and their own broken hearts because they had thought he was Messiah.

The disciples take a risk by being vulnerable, knowing that the traveler might ridicule their misguided devotion to a criminal. But instead the stranger comforts them by reminding them of messianic prophecies in the Scriptures, starting with Moses. The two might refuse to listen, but they are respectful and allow him to speak into their hearts, which later they will say burned within them when he opened the Scriptures (Luke 24:32). Yet it is their hospitality, their making a place for the other, that invites the moment of recognition. After they have prevailed upon the stranger to stay with them for a meal, he breaks the bread, and the two disciples see that this is their Messiah. The other, the stranger at their table is none other than the crucified Savior.

For our love to grow, it needs to grow beyond the self, even the self as loved by God. For God is holy Other as well as wholly with us. David Benner writes, "If we fail to recognize the other in people we encounter, we have no chance of discerning the presence of the Transcendent Other." Without that recognition, "the self must be its own god."[1]

There is a saying which reminds us that "the will of God is other people." Other people can be a doorway to God's presence as surely as prayer can be a doorway for us to speak and listen to Jesus Christ. Sometimes Christ's Spirit will enter despite our locked doors, but more often Jesus waits for us to open the door and let him in. We can provide hospitality for the encounter waiting at our own doorway to receive the other, or we can keep that door resolutely closed out of fear.

One reaction to the presence of the other is to form an opposing party called "us" and name the other "them." This allows us to control our fears and develop assumptions about the differences between us and them. These assumptions may or may not be true, but they form an effective barrier of defense. But our fear can also try to remake the other in our own image with a lens of sameness that blinds us to differences and refuses to see the possibilities of change that might come to us from acknowledging the other. In both cases dialogue and mutual listening become impossible, because with our mind made up, it is easy to label and stereotype. But a commitment to listen and dialogue with the other makes us available to one another and to God.

I taught a graduate course in spiritual direction for several years at a seminary. One semester a student sat in the back corner radiating her misgivings about my ability to teach her anything about prayer or spiritual companionship. I had misgivings of my own, because I would eventually have to meet with this student for one-on-one spiritual direction as well as endure her hostile presence in the classroom. On the morning I was to meet with her, I went swimming, as I often did before going to my office. Swimming those laps was always a time for solitude, and often for prayer as well. On this particular morning I carried my anxiety about meeting with my student into my workout. As I swam I heard the words *be quiet* as I reached out my arm, and then, a bit stronger, *shut up* as I lifted my head to breathe. I don't always receive such clear instructions, but this time the connection seemed evident, the instructions especially clear to my normally talkative self.

When I met with Angie that morning, I greeted her and then admitted that I knew nothing about her. She began to tell her story of growing up and now living in the tough Bronzeville neighborhood of Chicago. She told about her cruelly abusive stepfather, as well as the adult responsibilities she had to assume as a young child. She spoke about the challenges of raising her children in a violent neighborhood and her marriage with its difficulties and triumphs. She told me about her faith then and the way the church had sustained her but also frustrated her, and how God's presence was with her through it all. The only words I spoke were an almost involuntary "That sounds so hard!" as my own eyes filled. After she finished talking, she paused, looked at me and said, "That was not nearly as bad as I expected."

I was thankful for the early-morning wisdom I received. I sensed that this "not half bad" beginning might allow us to have a relationship. I also sensed that Angie had few safe places to tell her whole story from beginning to end. When she came back a second time, she was ready not only to talk but also to listen to me and to her own feelings. The third time she met with me, we spoke together for an hour. Then I left her alone in my office so that she could listen to God. When I returned an hour later, she was still there in the Spirit's presence and whispered to me, "I couldn't leave."

In Acts 8 the disciple Philip's question to the eunuch, "Do you understand what you are reading?" shares the same sense of simple curiosity. When the eunuch responds with his own question, "How can I, unless someone guides me?" Philip responds by explaining how this prophecy from Isaiah is related to the death and risen life of Jesus Christ. Then it is the eunuch's turn to ask yet another question: "What is to prevent me from being baptized?" Outwardly there seem to be a number of things that might prevent him from being baptized—his position as an outsider in Jewish society, his sexual status as a castrated male, his brief encounter with the story of Jesus, the lack of a proper confession of faith—but nevertheless, Philip listens and responds to the eunuch's own honest, open question by baptizing him.

In dialogue there is listening without judgment, assumptions or stereotype; there is listening for understanding rather than debate or even agreement; there is an atmosphere of safety and mutual respect. Often there is the sanctuary of silence. We might believe that Christian discipleship is rooted in teaching information—learning about the Bible or how to emulate Jesus' life. But it is really in listening rather than teaching that discipleship begins. Disciples sit at the feet of Jesus, listening to his words; disciples listen to the biblical words that not only are inspired but inspire as they are heard. Jesus' own ministry began by listening as he invited the first disciples to come to stay with him, as he asked them questions and listened for their response. What Jesus understood is that unless we listen first, no one is likely to hear us; unless we can hear another's heart or mind, they are not likely to listen to us. Love listens first.

Taking a Closer Look: Welcoming Others and Being Welcomed

While working as a social worker in Chicago, I was invited to a weekend retreat by one of my coworkers. When I arrived we were assigned to table "families." When we introduced ourselves, I realized that not just everyone at my table but everyone else in the room was Roman Catholic, and most were suburban women with large families. I was single and a Protestant Christian and lived in the city. Perhaps if it wasn't already evening and I had not come on the train to this less than desirable neighborhood, I might have turned around and gone out of the door. I had already made up my mind that I was not fitting into this group because they just would not understand me. But during that remarkable weekend, which was more like a party than a retreat, the women in my "family" became family. They knew nothing about my gifts or abilities, my accomplishments or failures. They loved me without reserve for those two and a half days. Their offering me a sense of belonging and acceptance deepened my own life in Christ. During the chapel time, I realized that if these women could love me just as I was, then God in Christ wanted to love me too, just as I was. I never saw those women again after that weekend. I don't even remember any of their names. But they had a remarkable influence on the rest of my life—my Christian life and my vocation.

There was mutuality in this community that was about finding connection where none might have seemed possible. There was a willingness to find the places where even our childhood stories of faith, which our own parents tried to convince us were so dissimilar, had some resonance. Now as adults we shared a similar frustration as we searched together for a truer sense of God's loving presence in our lives.

Most of us have known somebody who received us without criticism or judgment or even qualifications or questions. Take a closer look at your own life and see what gifts you received from those encounters as the other: What did it feel like for you to be the other, the outsider? Describe the situation and your feelings, thoughts and reflections. How did the sense of belonging change the way you saw yourself, others or God? How are those changes still alive in you? Where are you being asked not simply to be for something or someone but to be one with others?

Prayer Practice: Listening Stick

This practice can be done with two to four people in a small group. It is a practice in listening that can be done with acquaintances or strangers or friends. Undivided listening to others always leads to surprising both the listener and the receiver. If you are dividing a larger group into smaller groups, the leader might offer the beginning question.

Arrange chairs in a circle, sitting quite close—knee to knee if possible. Each group has an object such as a pen—we'll call it a listening stick—held by one person in the group.

If you are the person holding the stick, close your eyes, and for thirty seconds take an interior look, asking yourself what wants to be asked. This must be an honest, open-ended question. For example: What gives you joy? How do you respond to anger? What are you afraid of? How do you nurture your spirit? (These are just a few possible examples.) Then hand the stick to someone else and ask the question.

If you are the person receiving the listening stick, restate the question but personalize it—for example, "What gives me joy?"

Close your eyes and spend thirty seconds in silent reflection on the question. There is no right or wrong answer; there is no *answer*, simply your response. Notice your immediate response and then go deeper, trusting your intuition.

Open your eyes and speak to the group. Say whatever comes to your mind in response to the question. Take as much time as you need to say what needs to be said. Words might come slowly, and there might be pauses as you listen to your inner voice. You will know when you are done. It's a sense that there is no more to be said right now.

When you are finished go back inside yourself, again closing your eyes for thirty seconds, and ask: "What is the next question that needs to be asked?" This is not a linear exercise, so the question may or may not relate to what you've just said. Listen for the question without thinking about who will be responding to it. If just a phrase comes up, see if you can turn it into an open-ended question.

State the question—again, it needs to be open-ended just like the beginning question. Pass the listening stick to another person, who will respond to the question, repeating it and personalizing it.

Everyone else's role is just to listen as attentively as you can, pray for the person speaking, and notice how your own response might be very different or similar. Try to be as present to the person speaking as you are able, without responding to what has been said or ask a question. Instead practice undivided attention.[2]

If this listening practice is done in an atmosphere of respectful confidentiality, it not only gives an experience of deep listening but develops surprising community and connection. The listening stick makes us exercise the muscle of reflective listening to one another and also to our inner voice. One of the gifts of this practice is that you can completely set aside the voice inside that is mentally preparing a response. Because you do not know the question, you cannot formulate a response ahead of time. This allows you to be fully present to the person who is responding to a question. After you complete the practice, it is helpful to talk about the experience, asking what it was like or what you noticed about the practice, or what you heard.

Choosing Love

Some years ago a severely disabled woman asked me to be her spiritual director. She was a gift to me. Her slurred speech taught me to listen in a way I had not listened before. Her wisdom and intelligent discernment meant that I not only had to hear her but also needed to move quickly enough, spiritually and intellectually, to be able to *listen to* her. It was from her I learned both to hear and listen—to be able to say without embarrassment, "Is this what you meant?" or "Did I get this connection right?" She didn't mind if she had to repeat a word or a phrase, but she hated it when people pretended they understood her when they did not. When I met with her, I had to slow down to hear her but speed up to understand her. I had to adjust my ways to her ways in order to be able to listen.

I still get to practice this kind of listening as a volunteer at the Listening Post, a serene space in the noisy transit center of downtown Anchorage, Alaska (see www.listeningpostanchorage.com). Inside the transit center's first floor there is a cacophony of many people in varied circumstances trying to make it through the day, some homeless, most living on the edge. But just up the stairs, the Listening Post is a living room available to anyone who wants to come and sit. Volunteers listen to stories or just make space for a few quiet moments while people wait for the bus or come for a longer time of respite. Here everyone is treated with respect and confidentiality, and each person's presence is honored. The all-volunteer-run organization's philosophy is to provide an intentional listening space, believing that when people are heard without judgment, they begin to reclaim and express who they truly are.

In the L'Arche communities, those who are "normal" seek to simply live with rather than "do for" the disabled. There is a recognition of a shared wound, a brokenness and vulnerability, that the disabled and the able-bodied share. Randall, an assistant at an L'Arche community, describes it this way:

One of the things L'Arche has taught me is that we all have
brokenness that can never be fixed, no matter what other
people might do. Doctors, psychologists, and even clergy can't
fix us. In L'Arche there is a profound consensus regarding the
void and that only God can fill the void. Part of our role is to
help others come to realize that. In the process, you learn
about your own dark spots, some holes that can never be repaired. . . . The way of looking at reality, especially in America,
is that we're the best and brightest and we can find within
ourselves the resources to do anything we want to do. The
notion of humbly walking with God is pushed off on religious
freaks and people on the margins . . . there's a point where
there needs to be some reflection on our brokenness.[3]

When we listen to the stories of people with pain and realize
that we can do nothing about that pain, we touch our own
vulnerability. When we welcome the stranger, we welcome the
stranger who is within us. When we receive the broken outside,
we discover what is broken inside of us. By not protecting ourselves from our own weakness, we become open to finding
shelter together. "Transformation has to do with the way the
walls separating us from others and from our deepest self begin
to disappear. Between all fragile human beings stand walls built
on loneliness and the absence of God, walls built on fear—fear
that becomes depression or a compulsion to prove that we are
special."[4]

But there is also a secret at the heart of even the most disabled—a secret vocation that wants to be discovered. This vocation is primarily discovered at L'Arche in members' commitment to forgiveness and celebration. When forgiveness is not
just words but also an acknowledgment of shared pain, it can
flow into celebration. Founder Jean Vanier suggests a few es-

sential ingredients for celebration: good food and wine, seasoned with laughter.

Try to play stupid games—any sort. Let us come like children, to laugh and enjoy ourselves. This is what community should learn to do—to relax and to welcome people. And as it grows, it learns to know people, with their needs, their hopes, and their aspirations. Then it begins to accept, not judging or wanting people other than they are, but gradually discovering the music of their beings.[5]

What grows in the context of true community is a sense of abundance, a sense of knowing that who we are together is so much more than who we are as isolated people or even communities isolated from one another.

The Journey Center is an intentional Christ-centered spiritual center that welcomes people of all faiths, not simply to participate in its programs but also to share their own faith perspective in the community. Instead of spending energy articulating or discussing differences, this community is committed to finding bridges of understanding, caring and hospitality. This has made it a learning community, open to eclectic and diverse faith traditions but also learning to articulate what it means to be Christ-followers. In a part of northern California that often stereotypes churches as rigid and judgmental, the Journey Center model opens the door wide in the love of Christ (see www.journeycenter.org).

This is the kind of community that Jesus himself longed for with all those others that he met. "Jesus was not a man *for* others. He was one *with* others. . . . He *touched* the leper even before he got around to curing him. . . . Compassion is always, at its most authentic, about a shift from the cramped world of self-preoccupation into a more expansive place of fellowship, of true kinship."[6]

Jesus' vision of compassion isn't just about feeling the pain of the others or seeing the people on the margins but finding ways to dismantle those margins and be together. At the tables of the rich, he invited the poor; at the gatherings of the holy insiders, he welcomed the sinners; in the homes of the powerful, he received those who were considered least and last. At Christ's table he comes with the same compassionate hospitality and shares bread with us, inviting us to be his friends.

Living in Love by Receiving the Other

Listening to my life story. As you remember the story about the Center for AIDS Services, are you reminded of a place where you were surprised by hospitality and belonging? What was that like?

Listening to the biblical story. In Acts 8:26-39 Philip, listening to an angel of the Lord, is led to a wilderness road and an Ethiopian eunuch traveling on it. As you read the story, what examples of compassionate hospitality do you see in this story? In what ways is God hospitable and compassionate in this story as well?

Listening to love's continuing story. What is the difference between doing for others and being with others? How might your own encounters with others be different if you actively sought to be with them?

Further Reading

Boyle, Gregory. *Tattoos on the Heart: The Power of Boundless Compassion.* New York: Free Press, 2011.

Hauerwas, Stanley, and Jean Vanier. "The Vision of Jesus: Living Peaceably in a Wounded World." In *Living Gently in a Violent World: The Prophetic Witness of Weakness,* pp. 59-75. Downers Grove, IL: InterVarsity Press, 2008.

Taylor, Barbara Brown. "The Practice of Encountering Others." In *An Altar in the World,* pp. 87-105. New York: HarperOne, 2009.

3

Forgiving as We Are Forgiven

Learning to Love the Unlovable

*P*ulling herself up to her full three-year-old stature, my daughter made a parting demand that was both indignant and insistent: "I want my Real Mother!" She stalked off in a righteous, self-imposed exile to her bedroom, and I heard the door slam shut. I was surprised to find myself in weary agreement. I too wished for a Real Mother to appear, instead my own shabby self. In that desolate moment it was clear to her and to me that I was indeed not the Real Mother. And her absence was a grievous loss for us both.

Because on that rainy, dismal evening while preparing a dinner no one really wanted to eat, I needed the Real Mother myself. I needed her to care for me, and I needed her as someone to emulate. The Real Mother knows how to achieve the perfect balance of love and discipline, nurturing care and gifted restraint. The Real Mother bends but never breaks; she loves unconditionally but discriminately and carefully. She not only sees who her children are but sees just as effortlessly what they once were and what they could be. Her mothering is utterly unself-centered. I wanted with all that was within me to be the Real Mother not just for my three-year-old daughter but for my other two children as well. And I knew my daughter's longing. Because I had hoped that my own mother would be the Real Mother.

As a child I wondered how my mother, clearly a perfectionist in the art of homemaking, could be so lacking in the art of mothering. Apparently she was unable to see what was so obvious to me and all of my siblings: she let slide all of the best opportunities to be a Real Mother.

And the difficult truth is that she was just as profoundly disappointed herself that none of her daughters, though each attractive and clever in their own way, turned out to be the Real Daughter she had hoped for. Invariably, when my mother described a young woman in her community who was really "nice," the use of this word implied a negative contrast to one or all of her own four daughters. The repeated refrain of disappointment with its predictable country twang of regret was sung in an aggrieved voice. If a happier tune of mothers and daughters together thrummed quietly underneath it all, we rarely heard it. Instead we were caught up in a recurring loop of a dissonant *if only* that filled the space between us.

After my mother's death, we daughters went through her things, and I discovered an old pair of my mother's glasses—the glasses she wore at my own birth. I put them on and looked out her bedroom window, seeing across the street and beyond with perfect clarity. Her glasses were the same nearsighted prescription as my own. I took those glasses home with me, but despite their surprisingly trendy, retro style, I refused to wear them. What I had really seen that day was my mother's personal lens of disappointment, a prescription that was embedded in the way she saw those around her, including me. For me, wearing her glasses meant facing the truth that my mother had not been able to receive me for who I was but only as she wished me to be—a distortion no lens had been able to correct. When I first wrote about my mother, this seemed to be a necessary story, a simple acknowledgment of her distorted eyesight. But in a later rereading I feel my lack of generosity and just the faintest dark-brown taste of bitterness in my mouth. In my refusal to wear her glasses I read my own vanity and misperception of not only my mother but myself as well. What I understand now is not only my mother's failure to see me but my own inability to focus attention on her, as I remained caught up in looking at my own grievances. This reading brings me to the painful realization that she was no more able to be the mythical Real Mother to her daughter than I was to my own daughter. And in making this childish demand of her, I had held on to my personal grievances and withheld forgiveness. I had refused to acknowledge her struggle to love herself as well as those around her.

A colleague of mine frequently quotes Philo of Alexandria's saying "Be kind, for everyone you meet is fighting a great battle." My mother was fighting a great battle too, though it was inward and never spoken about. Who am I to continue to be at war with who she was and was not? After all, I can plainly see how I have disappointed and wounded my own children; I understand the need for kindness, even outright forgiveness. My own eyes have distortions that warp the true reality, that often keep me from recognizing the beauty directly in view. They settle for a surface understanding rather than real insight, and sometimes judge sarcastically. Perhaps discovering those glasses and our shared prescription was not a reminder that I can see things differently from my own mother. Perhaps instead those glasses reveal that I am not so different from her.

My mother is gone now and living, I believe, in a place where "no more tears" is not just the promise on a bottle of baby shampoo, but the reality that is heaven and home. But today I wonder if she is not most alive for me in that place where the search for the Real Mother with its inevitable sigh full of *if only* has been replaced by an acceptance of all that is. For it is finally, perhaps, in this clean letting go of the righteous Real Mother that my own mother can be seen for the gifted and intelligent person she was, a mother who struggled with loving well in the way that all of us struggle to love others. Then the Real Mother can be allowed her natural and inevitable death. And perhaps a bright, creative mom, who longed to give the best she knew to her daughters, might be revealed in all her glory.

The truth is that both of us mothers longed for kindness, not condemnation, blessing and not cursing. We both thought at times that we needed to do it all and do it well, to present the perfect offering of family and home to God and the world. And we both failed and felt our failure keenly. Our cycle of striving for perfection but feeling like failures left no room for words of kindness and blessing to be received or even believed. Worst of all, if the simple act of confessing our failures might fling us into that dark place of judgment and condemnation, how would it ever be possible for us to receive forgiveness, let alone give it to one another? By seeking after perfection or completion or wholeness or even holiness, we missed out on the entire kingdom of love that receives us as humanly imperfect.

God's gaze at both of us through the love of Jesus Christ is a look of loving forgiveness and sorrow. It holds love for who we are and sorrow for all the ways that we cannot embrace our God-created selves—human and imperfect but deemed worthy to share in God's story of forgiving sacrificial love in Jesus Christ. God's forgiveness is not dependent on my repentance, but if I fail to confess what I know to be true, forgiveness remains a beautiful gift unopened, not yet received into my life. Worse still, forgiveness is twisted into a sort of insult implying guilt for my having done something wrong when I myself claim no such truth. As with any good story, forgiveness cannot really be understood until we are willing to enter the narrative, to make the story not simply about a doctrine of justification but about a life of love.

In the novel *Saint Maybe*, author Anne Tyler tells the story of Ian Bedloe, who longs for forgiveness. In an adolescent mixture of anger and sexual attraction to his brother's new wife, Ian says words to his brother that have tragic consequences for his brother, his sister-in-law and himself as well. Ian, along with his aging parents, is left to care for three orphaned children, and his plans for his own future are changed forever. He is also left with an overwhelming sense of guilt as he finds out that not only did his words have enormous consequences but he was also wrong about what he offered as truth. At his sister-in-law's funeral, he yearns an end not to grief but to his guilt, and he feels a sense of relief as the pastor prays, "Let Thy mercy pour like a healing balm upon our hearts." Then Ian hears the congregation singing around him.

"The darkness deepens," they sang, "Lord, with me abide!" The voices ceased to be separate. They plaited themselves into a multistranded cord, and now it seemed the congregation was a single person—someone of great kindness and compassion, someone gentle and wise and forgiving. "In life, in death, O Lord," they finished, "abide with me." And then came the long, sighed "Amen." They sat down.

Ian sat, too. His knees were trembling. He felt that everything had been drained away from him, all the grief and
self-blame. He was limp and pure and pliant as an infant.
He was, in fact, born again.[1]

Perhaps we have heard Christian testimonies that have ended
at such a moment of deep feeling, but Ian soon admits that he
is unable to recapture this feeling of comfort and release. Still
searching, he wanders into a prayer meeting in a storefront faith
community called the Church of the Second Chance, and asks,
"Pray for me to be good again. . . . Pray for me to be forgiven."
But despite his hard work at caring for his brother's children, he
is unable to earn forgiveness. He becomes cautious and rule-
bound, trying to do and be good as he attempts to make amends.
When he complains to Reverend Emmett that he has been
"atoning and atoning" without feeling forgiven, the pastor reminds him that he needs to forgive as he is forgiven. He needs
to forgive his brother and sister-in-law.

Along the way Ian also discovers a deeper sense of grace than
all his efforts to relieve his guilt can supply. Eventually he looks
at the three children and acknowledges that "you could never
call it penance, to have to take care of these three. They were all
that gave his life color, and energy and . . . well, life." He also
discovers that the Church of the Second Chance and Reverend
Emmett are themselves learning to love beyond the rules and
make space for human imperfection. This too is a grace and a
gift for Ian. Finally, the children grown, Ian marries, and in preparation for the birth of his child, having long been a cabinet-
maker, he decides to craft a cradle. As he begins to work on it in
his woodshop, he realizes that he had always worked with
straight angles. "He had deliberately stayed away from the bow-
backed chairs and benches that required eye judgment, personal

opinion. Now he was surprised at how these two shallow U shapes satisfied his palm. . . . He took special pride in the cradle's nearly seamless joints, which would expand and contract in harmony and continue to stay tight through a hundred steamy summers and parched winters."[2]

And now his brother and sister-in-law reappear in Ian's imagination, not as victims of his careless words but as family. He looks at a picture of his sister-in-law Lucy and remembers her in her red bandanna, much younger than he himself is now. Then as Ian holds his own infant son, he remembers his brother Danny presenting his firstborn saying, "Here she is!" Ian receives them into the circle of love, not as victims of his guilt but as family. Forgiven, he now forgives them.

Theologian L. Gregory Jones notes that Tyler's story pictures forgiveness as a craft learned over time.[3] Woven into the story are two characteristics of the lifelong craft of forgiving as we are forgiven. The first is the realization that grace is alive in Ian's life, manifest not in his obedience to rules but in life with the three children who have ended up in his care, and with his parents. Forgiveness is part of a long healing process in his life, and in ours. As our relationship with God deepens, our understanding of how to live in relationship with God and one another grows. The heart of the matter is the daily practice of allowing God to love us, loving others and following Jesus in the way of the cross. Forgiving as we are forgiven is not about insisting on forgiveness that we may not be ready to either receive or give. It is learning to be with ourselves in our pain and learning to be with the pain of others.

The second characteristic of forgiveness is a letting go of the sharp edges and right angles of self-righteousness in order to embrace the softer curves of relational living, as we learn day by day to love God and those who are given to us. We cannot atone for our own sins or for the sins of others. What we can do is receive the gift of a life well lived and celebrate the way that redeeming love can come even when the worst happens to us. What we can do is "take the risk of offering words, gestures and actions that break the pattern of lovelessness for the sake of reconciliation."[4] Then we see that Light shining through even our bent and compromised lives.

When we say so confidently in the Lord's Prayer, "Forgive us our sins as we forgive those who sin against us," just what are we promising? It is almost as if what forgiveness means for us is the passing on of this gift of forgiveness to others—as we are forgiven, so we forgive. What if forgiveness is less about managing our own guilt and more about giving away the forgiveness that we've found in the death and resurrection of Jesus Christ? Perhaps forgiving others will mean entering their suffering, wounding and pain as well as our own, so that the Light can show through their cracks as well as ours. It may mean listening to both the victims and the perpetrators and seeing that we have knowingly and unknowingly shared in both roles.

The hard truth is that our fallen nature itself seems to move first toward getting even rather than forgiving; we are often more worried about fairness than about how we can live generously. Perhaps we've thought we needed this ability to survive. Choosing forgiveness will inevitably mean facing an inner resistance that screams, "This choice isn't fair!" Forgiveness is not cheap for God; it came at the price of his Son Jesus Christ's life. And there is cost for us, too, in choosing forgiveness. The cost is giving up the revenge that is due to us or those we love. It is allowing Christ to forgive through us. The apostle tells the Galatians, "It is no longer I who live, but it is Christ who lives in me" (2:20). By fully receiving and offering forgiveness, in the name of Jesus, we are birthing the life of Christ in us.

But can we really forgive? The Shoah, the Rwandan genocide, the killing fields of Cambodia, the senseless shooting of children in their own classrooms, the everyday sexual assault, abuse, even murder by family, friend and stranger seem to not allow for such a possibility. Many of these perpetrators are not even remorseful, let alone repentant. Some do not see what they have done as a wrong. Lacking a full and complete confession, we may consider justice best served by our tight hold on hatred and bitterness, rather than by finding another way.

Yet it is the remarkable nature of God's forgiveness that it comes to us even before our own repentance. Confession is simply the occasion for receiving forgiveness that has already been accomplished through Jesus Christ. The offer of forgiveness is itself an admission by the forgiver that a wrong has been committed. Embodying that forgiveness will mean an acknowledgment of the hurt inflicted and living out of its consequences.

Forgiveness is not forgetting. And it is especially important that an offense is remembered when there is a continued possibility of danger or harm. Forgiveness begins with remembering rightly and accurately and feeling the depth of our anger without turning it into hatred. But forgiveness means surrendering the right to get back at the other and eventually even giving up our anger or resentment.

Forgiving my mother took many years and is still incomplete. I know this is true. But I also know that forgiving her was not just about giving something to her, but about helping me to see that I need forgiveness as well. Sometimes we hold on to hurt in a way that blocks out the blessing of forgiveness for ourselves. My earlier refusal to forgive my mother left me without the grace I needed so much in my own life. Forgiving her in my own small way allows me to receive the infinitely larger, more expansive forgiveness of God in Jesus Christ.

Taking a Closer Look: Walking the Forgiveness Pathway
As you prayerfully walk this path of forgiveness, bring yourself and the perpetrator into the loving presence of God.

> *Remember* a hurt, a wound, a betrayal—a place where you have been let down, or hurt, dishonored, abused, lied to. Remember this place where you were diminished spiritually, emotionally, physically or spiritually. If you can, try to picture the person who harmed you; if you were betrayed by an institution or system, allow a picture of one person to symbolize this unjust institution. This happened—now name it, accepting it as tragic and true.
>
> *Remember* next your own brokenness—the pain and hurt that you might bear responsibility for, perhaps something that happened out of the hurt you experienced. When have you been selfish or dishonest, responding out of fear or anger or even hatred?
>
> *Remember* the brokenness of others—how are those who have hurt you like you in reacting to hurt or fear or anger or even hatred? They too are weak, wounded, imperfect human beings who get caught up in systems and patterns of hurt or abuse.
>
> *Acknowledge* a need for healing grace to be willing to forgive others and receive forgiveness yourself. Even though you might be willing to forgive, the power to forgive comes from God in Jesus Christ. This is the atonement that brings forgiveness and love to both the victim and the offender.

Invite God's healing power into your mind to heal your memories; invite God's healing power into your heart to heal your feelings; invite God's healing power into your body to lead you to acts of love rather than revenge.[5]

There is nothing magical or simple about this process of forgiveness. You are not pardoning or absolving someone by forgiving; nor are you condoning or excusing behavior. But you are giving up the right to get even; you are releasing resentments. As long as you hold on to hurts, they keep you in their grip, and your hands, your heart and your mind are not freed to receive love.

Each of these steps takes time. Do not hurry toward forgiveness, or the forgiveness that you offer and receive will be superficial and will not lead to true healing and transformation. You may need to hold on to a hurt or betrayal long enough to fully receive and experience its depth before you are able to let go and embrace your life with God as it is now, rather than as it was before.

Still, true forgiveness in Christ is meant to end the cycle of hurt and betrayal and bring a new beginning. By forgiving we enter the story of God's forgiveness in Jesus Christ with our own story of embracing pain, choosing love, letting go of revenge as an answer and forgiving others. This is what it means to live as Jesus lived and lives. Letting go does not deny the reality of pain. It means letting ourselves go through the pain with Christ while not trying to hide the hurt or wounding that has been inflicted on us. The resurrected Jesus was recognized by the nail holes in his hands and the spear wound in his side from his death on the cross. Those who have endured hurt and betrayal do not continue on as if it never happened; their lives continue to be experienced through those scars, even after the hurt is healed.

Prayer Practice: Praying the Lord's Prayer

The life of forgiveness is born of out of deepening relationship with God. In the Lord's Prayer Jesus is seeking to give us not "the right words for prayer" but his own relationship with the Father. When Jesus gave this prayer to his disciples, he was giving them "his own breath, his own life, his own prayer . . . his own understanding of his Father's purposes."[6] Though I was taught this prayer as a very young child (and taught it to my own young children) and frequently repeat it with the community in worship, I am still growing into the Lord's Prayer. Even for adults this prayer is "a bit like a child dressing up in his grown-up brother's suit, and having the cheek to impersonate him."[7] Growing into this prayer means living into my own history of wounding and woundedness in way that can get more rather than less difficult with time and circumstances.

Yet this is what the Lord's Prayer invites us to do—we are invited to be apprentices of Jesus as we live in a way that makes this prayer our own. Too often we recite the Lord's Prayer without meditating on our relationship with Jesus and the purpose that this prayer holds for us. As we pray "Forgive us our sins as we forgive those who sin against us," we are called to bring our prayer and our life together. We commit ourselves to incarnating the forgiveness of Christ in a dark and hurting world.

I want to offer a series of hand gestures to allow each petition to move from the head, where it so often remains, to the body, where it can become incarnate and find a home in your life. My suggestion is that you pray the Lord's Prayer with the hand gesture first and then speak the phrase.

Turn your hands up, giving thanks for all that they have held. Remember God's longing to hold your hand, to be in relationship with you. Gently lift your hands up toward God's presence and say,

Our Father who is in heaven

Bring your hands together with the fingers pointing upward, and make a small space between your hands. In that space, place a name for God that brings you close to God's heart. Then place your hands and that name over your heart. As you say the words, allow the words and the name to settle into your innermost being.

Hallowed be your name

Reach your right hand forward in a gesture of openness and trust.

Your kingdom come

Now reach your left hand forward, joining your will with God's intention and desire.

Your will be done

Let your outstretched arms form a circle, and gather in that circle those that you want to bring before God—both enemies and friends, and the whole fragile earth. As you gently lift this circle up into God's holy presence, knowing that it is all in God's care, say these words.

On earth as it is in heaven

Bringing your hands in closer to your body, letting them form a bowl to hold rice, the bread of much of the world, give thanks for food and for nourishment. Remember the hungry—those who hold empty rice bowls—as you plead.

Give us this day our daily bread

Bring your right hand up to your cheek without quite touching your hand to your face. Feel the warmth of your hand and recall God's gentle gift of forgiveness of the times you were wrong, hurtful or wounding.

Forgive us our sins

Take your left hand up to your other cheek, and again without touching, move it gently back and forth. Continue moving your hand gently and repeat the petition, now remembering that receiving forgiveness means sharing forgiveness and love with those who wound us.

As we forgive those who sin against us

With your arms at your sides, let your hands form tight, tense fists, feeling the way that sin can grip us. Now cross your arms over your chest. Repeat the words, this time feeling the weight of evil in our lives and the life of the world.

Lead us not into temptation

Let your arms unfold, and then slowly unclench your fists and feel the release. Say the words and let go of the weight of evil as you sense God's love and goodness releasing you.

But deliver us from evil

Raise your hands high, and let your body shout out God's greatness in these words of praise and blessing. Remember and know that you are praying to the One who is able to do more than we can ask or imagine.

For yours is the kingdom and the power and the glory forever

Choosing Love

In Matthew's Gospel, Jesus tells the story of a servant who owes a huge debt to his master. After pleading for understanding, the master forgives the small fortune he is owed. But later the master hears that this same servant has refused to forgive a small debt owed to him by another servant and has forced his fellow servant into debtor's prison. Appalled, he says to the servant he has forgiven, "You wicked slave! I forgave you all that debt because you pleaded with me. Should you not have had mercy on your fellow slave, as I had mercy on you?" Then the master takes back his mercy, reverses himself and puts the servant in prison. The grim warning at the end of this parable is clear: "So my heavenly Father will also do to every one of you, if you do not forgive your brother or sister from your heart" (Matthew 18:23-35).

Our unforgiveness does not cause God to take back his forgiveness, writes theologian Miroslav Volf, but "our unforgiveness may *just make manifest* that in fact we haven't allowed ourselves to receive God's pardon. . . . If, rather than being troubled by my inability to forgive, I don't want to forgive, there is a good chance that I haven't in fact received forgiveness from God, even if I believe that I have."[8] What the parable and Volf's commentary imply is that God's forgiveness of us in Jesus Christ is meant to birth a longing in us to forgive others. And if that longing or desire is not in us, then the gift of forgiveness has not yet been fully received.

When we are wronged, our first impulse may be to remember the wrong in a way that looks for a way to get even or at least allows us to fantasize about the vengeance the wrong deserves. But what if we chose to remember in a way that starts walking "in the footsteps of an enemy-loving God? How should I remember abuse as a person committed to loving the wrongdoer and overcoming evil with good?"[9] Volf asks this tough question in the context of an account of his own imprisonment and abusive interrogation as a Croatian Christian arrested by a Serbian communist who unjustly accuses him of being a spy. It is not simply a matter of remembering wrongdoing but of remembering in such a way that we do not return evil for evil.

Remembering rightly as Christ-followers will mean ending the cycle of abuse or betrayal or violence with our love. It will mean finding an alternative pathway that remembers but also is willing to let go. This is less a single act or offer than a journey walked with God.

The goal of forgiveness is not just removal of a personal sense of guilt. Rather, its "central goal is to reconcile, to restore communion with God, with one another, and with the whole creation."[10] While this might sound good, it is difficult for us to embody in the context of our day-to-day life. Even so, there are a few specific gifts that not only arise out of forgiveness but are necessary if we are to make forgiveness a way of life.

The first is to move from a willfulness that insists on its own rights to willingness. The willingness and openness to at least consider another perspective, another way of seeing, is the beginning of forgiveness. This availability makes it possible for us to ask God to bridge the space between the ones who wronged us and ourselves. It also moves us from stubborn unwillingness to face conflict and pain to understanding the distance that bitterness or anger has created between ourselves and the other. Allowing God's Spirit to be in this between-space provides each side a buffer of grace and gives us the possibility of reconciliation between the opposing sides. The Spirit's longing is to teach us mutual discernment and mutual confession and to release patterns of entrenchment and manipulation. The willingness to consider forgiveness and reconciliation is foundational to our call to love others as God loves us, to forgive others as God has forgiven us.

All this is from God, who reconciled us to himself through Christ, and has given us the ministry of reconciliation; that is, in Christ God was reconciling the world to himself, not counting their trespasses against them, and entrusting the message of reconciliation to us. (2 Corinthians 5:18-19)

There is another aspect to forgiveness as well. Forgiveness offers an entrance into a future of possibility and hope. French theologian Christian Duquoc says forgiveness is an "invitation to the imagination." While embracing forgiveness is not about forgetting the past, it is "the risk of a future other than that imposed by the past or by memory."[11] In his death on the cross Jesus offers us forgiveness by receiving our own sin and the world's evil. His resurrection offers us new life where condemnation and judgment do not have the last word. Jesus' forgiving love opens the door to hope in Christ.

Living in Love by Forgiving as We Are Forgiven

Listening to my story. Remember a time when you were forgiven. Did you find receiving forgiveness difficult or easy? What emotions did receiving forgiveness bring up for you? Now remembering a circumstance when you gave forgiveness. Was giving forgiveness difficult or easy? Why or why not?

Listening to the biblical story. In Matthew 18:21-22, Peter asks Jesus how many times he needs to forgive someone who has wronged him. This conversation introduces the parable of the unforgiving servant. How does the parable that follows answer or explain Peter's question regarding forgiveness? How does Jesus' answer and the story itself confirm or challenge your own understanding of forgiveness?

Listening to love's continuing story. How might forgiving someone as you are forgiven be an "invitation to the imagination"? What does it mean for you to be given a ministry or message of reconciliation because God has "reconciled us to himself through Christ" (2 Corinthians 5:18-19)?

Further Reading

Jones, L. Gregory. "Forgiveness." In *Practicing Our Faith: A Way of Life for a Searching People,* edited by Dorothy Bass, pp. 133-48. San Francisco: Jossey-Bass, 1997.

Volf, Miroslav. "God the Forgiver" and "How Should We Forgive? How Can We Forgive?" In *Free of Charge: Giving and Forgiving in a Culture Stripped of Grace,* pp. 121-224. Grand Rapids: Zondervan, 2005.

PART TWO

Choosing Faith

4

Following Jesus

Learning the Language of Desire

Shortly after moving to Anchorage, Alaska, I was invited to be part of a retreat leadership team. During that retreat week, one of the other leaders invited us to listen imaginatively to a story of Jesus with his disciples in Mark 6:45-51. He told us to picture the events, smell the smells, touch and taste, hear and see it all as the story unfolded. Then he said, "In your mind's eye, allow yourself to actually be in this story, while keeping your eyes on Jesus."

As this story begins, Jesus tells his disciples to go into the boat ahead of him to Bethsaida. Then he goes up on a mountainside to pray. When evening comes, the boat is in the middle of the lake, while Jesus is on land. From the place where Jesus stands, he can see the disciples straining to pull the oars, because a storm has come up and the wind is against them. In the darkness before the dawn Jesus comes down from the mountain and walks across the water, coming toward them.

Now I can see myself too, one of those disciples in the boat, pulling as hard as I can on the oars, fighting the wind and the current. From my position in the boat I see Jesus coming across the water toward us. But then the gospel story says that Jesus "intended to pass them by" (Mark 6:48). As the writer describes the disciples' fear, as they believe Jesus to be a ghost, I feel another emotion altogether. I feel anger. After all, doesn't Jesus see how hard all of us in the boat are struggling to keep it afloat? Doesn't he care that the wind is pushing against us so hard? Why is he about to pass us by? It feels outrageous that all of us, including me, are about to be ignored by Jesus. For me the story ends right there, as Jesus intends to pass me by.

Every time I remember the phrase "intended to pass them by," I feel my anger toward Jesus surge. Finally, I ask a wise friend to let me talk with him about my reaction to Jesus, which seems out of all proportion to the simple story itself. He listens intently to my story and my angry feelings, but then asks me nothing about the story itself or my role in it. Instead he asks me to describe what life is like for me now that I've moved from Chicago, Illinois, to Anchorage, Alaska. "How have things changed since your move?"

I reply, "In Chicago I was always busy; there were lots of outward pressures of classes and responsibilities built into my daily life. In fact, everyone seemed required to be busy all of the time. And I certainly shared in that hectic culture. In Anchorage I don't seem to be required to do so many things as in Chicago. In fact, I'd say that though I still have good work to do, it is not so outwardly motivated by others."

Then he asks, "What's that like for you, Helen?"

"Well, the truth is, it is a bit scary for me," I answer. "I'm accustomed to my life being about meeting the demands of others—the things I ought to do and should do. But most of my work in Alaska needs to be interiorly motivated, as I work at caring for my students online in my own home, or meeting with people for spiritual direction or writing. Part me finds this exciting; another part of me is terrified that without the outward demands I will fail, neither continuing my work nor being asked anywhere to teach or write or offer spiritual direction, and my sense of calling or vocation will be lost."

As I speak these words, I feel my anger crumbling around the crippling sense of fear it has masked. I remember again my companions in the boat, who were not so scared of the storm; they knew how to weather it because it was just that, weather—life's familiar burden in the middle of the lake. But they were terrified at the appearance of Jesus walking on the water.

My friend asks another question that changes my perspective on where I live now and where I had been living. "I wonder if the boat where you are struggling against the wind, working so hard with those oars, is your life in Chicago that you've already left behind. Perhaps Jesus is inviting you to get out of the boat and follow him as he moves on the water." As soon as he says this, I can feel the truth of his observation. And I realize that what I need to hear are Jesus' words to me, "Take heart, Helen, it is I; do not be afraid," the very words that Jesus called out to his frightened disciples (Mark 6:50).

It is so simple but I couldn't see it, because I was holding on to how I thought things "ought" to be instead of following Jesus toward a new reality. If I got out of the boat, I could leave that struggle behind and follow Jesus into the stillness of the place I now called home. Facing my fears meant leaving behind the boatload of expectations that came from others. By following Jesus out of the boat, I was entrusted with my own life, the life I had longed for all along. My friend had simply stated the obvious. Hearing his words, I knew I wanted to follow Jesus out of that boat and into my own life in Christ.

There exists in the Christian community the misperception that
what we want will surely be at odds with God's will. While this
may be true at the earliest stage of faith, we often hang on to the
idea that God will ask us to do something, go somewhere, that
will be totally at odds with our nature or our abilities or our own
wants. But what if this is not true? At best it may be an excuse,
at worst an outright lie, that keeps us from articulating our
hopes and dreams, our longings and desires, even our dissatisfaction. After all, God created us with all of those gifts and abilities, those longings and desires.

It is surprising how often the question Jesus asks of his followers is, "What do you want?" When Jesus sees the disciples
of John following him, he turns around and asks them, "What
are you looking for?" (John 1:38). When Jesus sees the man
lying at the pool of Bethesda, he says to him, "Do you want to
be made well?" (John 5:6). As he walks to Jericho, Jesus stops
when he hears the blind man call out, looks down at Bartimaeus
and asks, "What do you want me to do for you?" (Mark 10:51).
Even his words to the rich young man encouraging him to give
up everything and follow Jesus held the implicit question, "What
do you truly want?" (see Luke 18:22).

Sometimes it seems that the answer is obvious. What blind
man would not want to see? What paralytic would not want to
be healed? But those judgments are easier to make when we are
standing outside of their particular life circumstances. When we
actually see through the eyes of a man blind since birth, or lie
on the mat with someone who has been there for thirty-eight
years, or feel the power of a ruler who has amassed not simply
wealth but also social stature, the weight of the question and its
answer seem far less obvious.

What God touches in the Jesus question "What do you want?"
is the relational dynamic of longing, desire and even dissatis-

faction at the heart of our lives. Perhaps dissatisfaction and desire are a realistic response to our world so incomplete in love and compassion—or as I experienced my own life, so lost in my performance that I couldn't even see Jesus calling me to follow. Australian monk Michael Casey writes that at "a very deep level of our spirits, we seem to have a memory of something better. Children born in a refugee camp may be delighted at a poor meal; less so their elders who remember better days."[1] That desire for the More that we perceive only dimly, but at times sense, is meant to move us toward all the More that is beyond in God.

Jesus speaks to this desire in the language in which people are able to receive it—or not. Children are received into the kingdom with the language of loving touch and blessing. Rather than urge them away, Jesus holds them up as models for kingdom life. The wealthy religious leader asks what he might do to "inherit eternal life," and Jesus answers him in the dialect of possession and ownership, telling him he must let go of all his material treasure to follow Jesus and "own" eternal life. When the blind man responds to Jesus by asking for his sight, he receives the healing he longs for but also receives an invitation to get up and be with Jesus along the way as a disciple, a follower. He already understood who Jesus was, but he needed his sight to follow him. Zacchaeus, the rejected tax collector, longing to simply see Jesus, is told that he is to be the host, receiving Jesus in his own home so that he can be known by Jesus. Hidden in these conversations is the longing to be held and received, to find true life, to see and follow, to be known and to belong.

This longing for the More can be painfully apparent in our dissatisfaction, but it can also appear "as a deep energy, as something beautiful, as an inexorable pull, more important than anything else inside us, toward love, beauty, creativity and a future beyond our limited present."[2] Most of us have at least had a glimpse of that pull toward transcendence. Often these glimpses come in seemingly insignificant moments when we sense that just now, we are exactly at one with ourselves and God in who we are and what we are doing, or even not doing.

A preschool teacher told me of a moment like that as she bent down to tie the shoe of a toddler and smiled, knowing this good work was filled with God's blessing. Rereading a devotional for church planters that he himself had written, a pastor described how his eyes welled up because he knew what he had written was true and good. Teaching spiritual formation in Anchorage for Multnomah Biblical Seminary, I stood at a whiteboard learning together with my four gifted students, and thought, *This is what I love.* After putting on a birthday dinner for her daughter and seeing her daughters' friends having a good time, author Ruth Haley Barton wrote: "This is my best self. This is who I want to be more and more by God's grace. These are the moments that I will remember on my deathbed and say, 'That was what I was meant for.'" Later she describes this as a moment when she was fully present to God and to others in love.[3]

What do *you* want? Important as this question is, it can feel dangerous. What if what we want is not right for us, or just plain wrong? How can we sort out our own longings from all the advice we hear—what we've learned from parents or teachers or pastors or spouse or friends? And isn't the question itself just a little bit selfish, maybe even having a sense of narcissism at its core? Wouldn't it be better to follow right behavior or right doctrine or at least right thinking or feeling? Correctness—political or religious or ethical correctness—seems easier to define; it seems easier to draw the boundaries of right and wrong, inside and outside, true and false.

We settle for a focus on the outward life, rather than an interior life that is directed toward our core values, purpose or freedom. In a culture focused on things that can be bought, driven, worn or consumed, there is plenty of outer stuff to settle for. The wedding registry suggests the exact model of blender or toaster we want to receive, but not what our marriage will need in terms of forgiveness, patience and self-control. Or we just settle for relieving the pain or discomfort of life—a symptom of a deeper healing that might be needed. To actually name what we want, our true desire, might well mean facing hurt and pain. It will almost certainly require us to listen to ourselves at a deep level. It's easier to simply relieve the experience of pain without discerning the cause or seeing the need for healing.

Another reason for settling for something less is that these core desires can be safely hidden under a shell of conformity to the mores of culture, job, family or even church. It is easier to wear this mask of conformity designed to fit the requirements of others and avoid answering the Jesus question, "What do you want?" It is simpler not to rock the boat, to just sit quietly and do as we are told. Why question long-held beliefs about life that allow us to survive in a challenging world? Still, the failure to answer this question leaves us living a life that is dry, brittle and ultimately deadening.

When we live out of our deepest longings, these desires become attached to God's own desire for us. When we name our dissatisfaction and glimpse God's desire for us, the power of that joint longing fuels faith's following of Jesus. If we can name our deepest desires, God wants them for us as well. In fact they will guide us to who we were created to be in Christ and with Christ. But recognizing our dissatisfaction and our longings will mean facing the impossibility of achieving them on our own.

This is a difficult realization and perhaps what keeps us settling for lesser desires that are disordered and do not lead us
toward God, or conditional desires that are not true, or superficial desires that are distractions. Far from being selfish, naming
our deepest desire means facing our human limits, as our desires
always exceed our resources. Casey insists that this is "not ineffective workmanship on God's part, but an indication of our
destiny and the means to reach it. We were made for self-
transcendence. To pretend otherwise is to live a lie."[4]

Following Jesus Christ is about becoming fully alive in Christ.
It is not about settling for less than we hoped; it is about longing
for More—living and praying our way through all the ways we
may have settled until we see the truth. Life in Christ itself is
meant to lead us into truth; it is never a denial of reality. But
naming our true desires is more than naming where we missed
the mark. In its longing for fullness of being, it is "like the sun
warming a seed into life, like the work of clearing away weeds
and bringing water to the interior garden of St. Teresa's inspired
imagery."[5] Like those seeds, we may need to allow God to love
our shallow selves by naming even our disordered longings in
God's presence until, by God's grace, the deepest desire is revealed. Only then will God's own soil, watering and light reveal
our interior garden.

Sometimes it is easier to live even a difficult life than to claim
the freedom of living fully in the grace of Jesus Christ. Growing
up in my childhood church, I heard God's grace preached from
the pulpit at church on Sunday. But the other six days we lived
a kind of "works righteousness" that allowed little room for
grace to appear, even if we had thought we deserved the amazing
grace that we sang about on Sunday. It was easy for productivity
to be our personal justification, even when we were taught about
justification by faith in Christ as a gift of God. Perhaps Jesus

came to us as we hoarded our riches of good works and offered us the opportunity to leave everything and follow him. But we looked at him sadly and reminded him of the work still to be done, the ministry to be accomplished, the difficulty, really the impossibility, of leaving it all behind to follow him.

It is not a simple choice for us to get out of our boat and trust Jesus with our life, to leave our mat behind and let go of our accustomed way of life. Until we become restless and dissatisfied with what we have settled for, we will resist the call to follow Jesus into our heart's desire. Until we are discontent with the way things are we may not choose to search out what we truly want.

We must come to understand that the residual dissatisfaction with life as we have shaped it for ourselves is the very essence of what we name "call." Clearly, it is at the moments of dissatisfaction with life as we know it now that the door to the future swings open for us. There is something missing in the making of who we are meant to be that we are being goaded to pursue.[6]

If we are persistent in letting Jesus ask, "What do you want?" in the context of our own life, we can also be confident that God will sort our trivial or even wrong-headed desires into his truth. God treasures our longing for finding our way to an unfamiliar place without getting lost, because it is a desire for finding not simply the way but the Way. Even a parking-place prayer is prayer into the messiness of our lives, the longing for order in our personal chaos. Rarely, however, do we stay with these surface desires long enough to see the deeper dissatisfaction with how we live that they express. God is able to sort out our desires, if only we will keep seeking the answer to the Jesus question—what do you want?

Taking a Closer Look: Counting the Cost

A story is told of a woman who went to a store that sold unusual merchandise, a place where there were desires and values on the shelves as well as dreams and longings. The woman spent a long time choosing a few items, being careful not to appear greedy, before she made her way to the counter. She gently carried her items—a sense of personal peace, freedom to be the person she longed to be—to the checkout. As she laid these precious gifts carefully on the counter, she was surprised to see that the clerk was Jesus himself. Treating her choices with the same care she had, Jesus looked at them.

Then Jesus told her that her money would not purchase the items she had chosen. Instead she would have to give something away if she wanted to receive the item. For that sense of peace she longed for, she might have to pay with her cherished bitterness. For that freedom, she might have to uncover her childhood shame and be willing to offer it. The woman stared for a long while at the gifts she had chosen for herself, but in the end she put them back on the shelf.[7]

Imagine yourself in this same store. What items might you take off the shelf? What do you want—a sense of belonging, to be known and accepted, to feel at home with others, to find peace in your family—or do you want to be healed of hurts, be forgiven for your past, be reconciled with a brother or sister, a parent or a friend, or is there something else? Take some time to reflect on what you truly want, where your deepest desire or strongest dissatisfaction lives. When you are ready bring it to the counter, see that Jesus is there, willing to give you what you want. But he is asking for something from you in exchange. What must you let go of to receive your heart's desire? What will you carry with you as you leave the store?

Prayer Practice: Praying with Jesus

If our truest desire is to follow Jesus, then we must accept Jesus' invitation to be his friend. Friendship is not about following the rules; it is not even about mirroring the movements of Jesus. It is about living our lives fully with him. It is about choosing to spend time with him. We do this is by reading about Jesus and seeing who he is and how he acts. But we remain observers of the life of Jesus until we join our lives with his in friendship. An intimate relationship demands the back and forth of listening and mutual self-disclosure.

One way of doing this is through imaginative meditation on a gospel story that attracts us, a story that holds a view of Jesus that catches our attention. This is not about finding the "right" story, but a story with a specific setting, emotions and a sensory presence is easier to enter into. Some of our earliest learning happened through the imagination of story and play. When we enter a story this way we don't exit our adult self or our reason, but we allow our imagination to invite us into the story itself. When I watch a movie that captivates me, I am involved imaginatively. When I read a novel that is true to itself, I see the characters in their own setting. So too the gospel stories are meant to be read with our God-given imagination.

Before you react by saying that you don't have an imagination, notice what you feel when I suggest that you cut open a lemon and bite into it. That's your imagination letting you know how your body will react to the sour taste. Or remember the way your eyes filled with tears when you heard a sad story or your heart was moved by love's gesture. But not all of our imaginations are alike. Some of us can get a feel or sense of a person, while others remember the particular tone of voice or their earthy smell, or hear their raucous laugh. When you pray with Jesus, use the gifts of imagination that are yours—not what you think or imagine are the gifts of others. Like an unused muscle, imagination can grow just as reason does with exercise.

This prayer begins with your own desire to know Jesus intimately as friend to friend, and trusting Christ's Spirit to direct your imagination. Read the biblical passage several times until you are comfortable with the story. Then allow the story to unfold in the here and now, and let yourself be an active participant if you can. If you find this difficult, imagine that you are telling the story to a child, keeping it active and alive. Allow yourself the freedom to bring the facts close to home. Perhaps the good Samaritan will be traveling on a bicycle in the downtown of your own community, or the boat with the disciples will be on a stormy Lake Michigan as mine was. Now let it unfold—notice where Jesus is and where you are in this story. Are you a bystander or a disciple or lying alongside the road waiting to be healed? Let yourself dialogue especially with Jesus about what you are experiencing. After you feel that you are finished with your prayer, at least for now, end with the Lord's Prayer. This grounds your imagination in the prayer Jesus taught all of his disciples to pray.

In describing imaginative prayer, author Margaret Silf says there are two rules that must be followed: "Never moralize or judge yourself. Always respond from your heart and not from your head."[8] She admits herself that these are not easy to follow, because we all carry within the inner critic, quick to defend or condemn or analyze or exhort. But do be aware of the voice of your heart—feelings and reactions—just as you would in a human relationship. Even if they feel negative, those reactions can be an indicator of something deeper, just as my own anger had fear underneath it when I saw Jesus pass the disciples (and me) by. Jesus can be both a comforting friend and a challenging companion.

There are often concerns about trusting the imagination, and these are understandable. It is wise to be cautious, checking your imaginative prayer in reference to your own past experience, God's nature in the Bible and your faith community. Because this prayer is personal and unique, it is good to share it with a trusted friend. Even recounting the prayer can help you to see deeper meanings and connections pointing you toward God.

However, this prayer allows the gospel story to retain its characteristic narrative style and the Bible itself to remain alive. These stories are meant to engage our hearts and minds so we can come to know, love and follow Jesus, not as servants but as friends. Getting to know Jesus this way can be challenging as well as comforting, but it is back-and-forth dialogue that builds the friendship and makes it real. Such an invitation to follow Jesus is not about just changed behavior but joining with Christ, being loved by him and loving what he loves.

Choosing Faith

Having sensed an invitation to invite others to join with Christ, Pastor Kent Carlson gathered together a small group of people and began Oak Hills Church. After a rewarding beginning, Oak Hills Church continued to grow, attracting people to its Sunday seeker service and other programs. The church became so outwardly successful that Pastor Carlson was invited to speak at a national church conference highlighting large, growing churches. But just ten years after its beginning, the staff at Oak Hills Church began to question the church's mission, wondering where they had lost their original intention of helping everyone in the church be fully alive in Christ.

As they talked at a staff retreat, they realized how dissatisfied they were with the ministry of the church. The staff felt that instead of experiencing joy or a sense of fulfillment, they had created a monster that required constant feeding. They realized the way they were doing church by attracting people as consumers was in direct conflict with Jesus' warning that we would have to lose our lives in order to find them. They began to recognize that in faithfulness to the gospel of Jesus Christ, they needed to acknowledge that "consumerism was not a force to be harnessed but an anti-biblical value system that had to be prophetically challenged."[9]

When the pastors of Oak Hills Church became dissatisfied with their professed life in Christ and chose to stop feeding the "monster" of church consumerism, there were serious costs in membership, staffing, finances and even their standing as a "growing, successful" church among other large churches. They had to shift their intention and focus away from meeting demands and concentrate instead on being formed as the body of Christ, both individually and as a community.

The story of Oak Hills Church is really the challenge facing each of us as well. Finding an authentic life in Christ seems attractive and even enjoyable, certainly rewarding, until we realize that it will mean refusing to feed whatever "monsters" we have trusted instead of Jesus to give us life. Our attachment to Christ will remain sentimental and superficial unless it faces the dissatisfaction with life as it is and the desire for the More that lies underneath our surface desires. Following Christ is always a journey into truth; it is never a denial of reality. This is not a life we create but a life that is discovered out of and in the life that we are given. Any other external gratification is just an illusion; it is not journeying with Jesus.

This is a life-giving Way, but it is also our choice. Living in Christ is choosing to walk with Jesus as the Way and leaving lesser ways behind. That choice was a painful one for the Oak Hills congregation and staff, because it meant leaving some of their outward sense of success behind to find a truly Christ-centered community. The pastors at Oak Hills realized that even though transformation is the work of the Holy Spirit in us, the Spirit will not overwhelm us to get the work done. Instead we "have to want it."[10]

Naming our true longing will mean being as honest as we are able to be. It will mean being willing to change direction rather than stubbornly pushing forward. It will mean staying long enough with our wants to see what lies beneath the surface. Still, no amount of personal determination fueled by effort will bring any real transformation. What is needed instead is availability and openness to God's invitation as our heart's desires become aligned with God's desires. Our role as Christ-followers has more to do with "consent than initiative . . . most simply saying yes to God's invitation to loving encounter."[11] When Jesus encounters people, what he asks of them is the honesty and the willingness to bring their true selves, even when that true self is blind or sick, dishonest or frightened. This was true in the Gospels and it is equally true today. Honesty with God is not about just avoiding lies but a radical openness, an availability to choose the More and leave lesser choices behind.

But clarifying our true desire also helps us to see what the heart of the matter is for us. When a family clarifies its desire to spend time together, sacrificing personal computer time feels more like a joyful choice than a loss. In her cookbook *More with Less,* Doris Janzen Longacre emphasizes how less can really be more: "Cutting back sounds like a dismal prospect. 'Let's splurge, just this once' appeals to North American ears. Put dismal thoughts aside then, because this book is not about cutting back. This book is about living joyfully, richly, and creatively."[12] When you choose to prepare food together and eat it with others, that choice changes your perspective on sacrifices of time and even food choice. Realizing the More makes you realize how much less your other priorities might be.

God's own agenda for us is actually much more radical than most of us expect. Jesus invited the disciples to come with him to "the place where I am going." When Thomas questioned him saying, "Lord, we do not where you are going. How can we know the way?" Jesus said to him, "I am the way, and the truth, and the life" (John 14:4-6). Jesus says that if you want to find the way to God, you will need to choose him as the Way. While we might simply settle for choosing the right thing, "God's agenda is much grander. God wants us to choose the right *way*."[13] It is this Way, this Life, this Truth that will lead to a self in Christ that is motivated by love and attached to God through Jesus Christ.

Living in Faith by Learning the Language of Desire

Listening to my life story. When have you been invited out of the boat of your known experience or security or expectations to follow Jesus? How was that invitation a journey of faith for you? What do you notice now about "leaving the boat" that you did not understand then?

Listening to the biblical story. In Luke 18:35-43, Jesus stops along the road to respond to someone's cry and asks a question. Hear this story again, and with your imagination "see" the story in your mind's eye. Notice the road, the crowd, the beggar and especially the gaze of Jesus as he stops and asks his question. What is stirred in you as you hear this question from Jesus? Whether you feel challenged or comforted, puzzled or excited, allow a conversation with the risen Jesus to unfold, speaking friend to friend.

Listening to faith's continuing story. Where are you dissatisfied or longing for more in your life with God? What might it mean for you to embrace your "best self" and fully receive the gift of faith in your life? How might this affect your relationship with God or those around you?

Further Reading

Casey, Michael. "The Human Basis of Prayer." In *Toward God: The Ancient Wisdom of Western Prayer,* pp. 11-23. Liguori, MO: Triumph Books, 1996.

Silf, Margaret. *Inner Compass: An Invitation to Ignatian Spirituality.* Chicago: Loyola, 1997.

5

Embracing Vulnerability

Finding Strength in Weakness

I was standing next to the crib where my nearly newborn child lay when a passerby asked, "Is this your first child?"

"No," I replied, "this is my third child."

"Well, then," she said, "this must be old hat to you," waving her hand casually around the pediatric intensive care unit of Oakland Children's Hospital.

I looked down at my infant son lying still in the crib, his tiny arms pinned to the mattress, tubes running in and out of his little feet, and the tiniest oxygen cannula inserted in his nose to give him the extra air he needed just to live. I was wordless, unable to respond at all. There was nothing about the past sixteen hours that had felt "old hat" or even understandable in any way that I had experienced before.

I had not expected that my newborn would catch a cold when I took him on an outing with my older son's kindergarten class. As I look back now, it seems obviously foolish, high-risk, even borderline abusive behavior for a mother. But then it was no

more than I had done with my two older children. I had not
known that I should have called 911 in the middle of the night
instead of waiting until morning to call the doctor. I hadn't
known that when my baby stopped nursing so that he could give
his total effort to merely breathing, he was in an acute physical
crisis. Nor had I known that as I drove him the six blocks from
the pediatric office to the emergency room, even this effort
would be too much for his tiny lungs, and his shallow breathing
would nearly stop altogether.

When I lifted my own baby out of the car seat, I no longer
knew this clammy, blue-gray stranger. As the emergency room
secretary handed me a sheaf of admission forms, I offered up my
child with outstretched arms, thinking, *Here, take, and receive
my baby.* Because I knew that if he remained in his own mother's
arms for even a few more minutes, he would surely die.

Just at that moment, somebody stepped out of the emergency
room itself and took the baby out of my arms and into her own
medically competent hands. I did not even see her face but willingly released my newborn son into her care. Another somebody
led me away to an empty room down the hall, where I sat alone
and waited to hear whether my child would live—or not. I remember the room itself as an ordinary room turned into what
felt like a jail cell, littered with old *Better Homes and Gardens*
magazines on the coffee table to distract the accused. I remember
it as a confessional box with no priest available to the hopeless
sinner sitting on the orange plastic couch.

No, a priest did not arrive until the following day. My priest
was the nurse from the same emergency room, making a follow-
up visit to the pediatric intensive care unit. My voice broke as I
look at her and whispered, "You saved my baby's life. I didn't
know anything. He nearly died in my care. He surely would have
died if you had not taken him away from me."

I paused then, waiting for the accusing gaze, the words of condemnation I surely deserved for my failure as a mother. Instead, she simply waved her hand around this room full of fierce suffering, in a gesture of experienced knowing. She said, "It is easy to second-guess everything once you end up here. But for you now as a mother, the most important thing is not what you could have done and didn't do, or what you should not have done and did do. The most important thing is that you have a beautiful infant son, and he is alive and needs your care and love."

Then we both looked down at my baby, my own child whose cheeks were already looking less gray, whose narrow face was now a bit less gaunt. We were awed by how lovely he was at that moment. After gazing for another silent moment at my son, I looked back at the nurse from a place beyond speech. Tears were all I had to offer in response to such fathomless compassion for me, for my baby.

It was a long time before I could speak at all about my near-death experience with Jesse, and then it was only in the halting, monosyllabic way of the nearly mute. Now I think I was afraid that I could not speak about it without returning to the terror of that time. And then the awful fear and failure would grip me in the gut again, and I would find myself back in the belly of the whale. But it was holding it inside without acknowledging the fear and failure that sent me back into the belly of the whale over and over again. At those times I threw myself overboard and was swallowed up whole, convinced that this was just punishment for my many near-misses as a mom, as a wife, as a teacher and pastor and spiritual director, as a human being. I willingly threw myself overboard rather than name my sense of condemnation and loss.

My son Jesse was a teenager before I was able to write this story down. Perhaps I just didn't want to face my story of a near-death mother-failure. But it was only when I wrote into my fear that I was able to remember the compassion of that nameless nurse who offered Jesse back into my flawed care. Only then was I able to receive all that experience held for me about my own vulnerability and the fragility of life. Receiving that story into my life also regifted me with my own lanky teenage son, who could so easily annoy and frustrate me. But most of all, it relieved the burden of the "not-good-enough" mother that I had unknowingly carried all those years. Sometimes we can carry for years our role as victim or offender, the one who was hurt or the one who did the hurting, and words of forgiveness can slide right off the thick skins that we develop for living out those character roles.

Sometimes I wonder why I practice a faith that seems to be beside the point in so much of contemporary life. But when I can find the courage to remember the worst, or when the worst finds me, I remember too the keening need in that place for a table where the useless magazines filled with household hints and sporting statistics are swept away with a mighty arm and an outstretched hand. And the longing to find there instead a chipped chalice with traces of blood at the bottom, the dregs of presence. But sharing that chalice with Jesus means we must embrace our human vulnerability—all the ways that we are not enough or count ourselves weak or even a failure.

Without this acceptance of the real in our lives, Christian faith can become a mask we wear and a way to distance ourselves from a threatening reality with pious phrases. But true faith in God is never a denial of reality, but a gift from God large enough to hold even the most painful of human realities. It grows best when we are most honest, hiding nothing from ourselves or God. And it shrivels when we refuse to let go of illusions of control or rationalizations about our imperfections. The frank acknowledgment that the Lord's compassion comes to us not because of any accomplishments but because "he remembers that we are dust" (Psalm 103:14) is meant not as judgment but as sweet relief for those who have been striving to maintain a facade of personal righteousness.

Taking a Closer Look: Writing or Drawing into My Fear

Perhaps there is something that remains in the closet in your otherwise upstanding life. Perhaps it is not "nice" or "right" by some definition, even though deep within you know it is true about you. I find as a journaling teacher that sometimes a fear that our secret places will be uncovered means we never write or speak about them at all. And then we are silenced.

We may easily sing the words "Amazing grace . . . that saved a wretch like me," but it is the identification of us as wretches that rings loudly and long, rather than the clear invitation of grace. Unless we surrender our fear or our anger, even our bitterness or despair, words about God's loving presence within us can seem to be a fantasy; assurances about the offer of grace can feel like a hoax.

Begin by writing a question at the top of page of blank paper, and then answer with words or pictures without pausing to think or reflect. As you flow-write or draw, allow yourself the freedom to say it all, knowing that no one will ever read or see this paper. You can rip it up into tiny pieces after you finish, or burn it into a pile of ashes. If you get stuck, try writing or drawing with your nondominant hand because sometimes it can connect more easily with the self that lives below our everyday awareness. Remember that no one is going to read this and you are free to destroy it after you journal. If this feels overwhelming, you may want to set a timer for ten minutes and just write or draw until the timer gives you permission to stop.

This is the question: What are you afraid someone will find out about you?

Now personalize that question and write it at the top of your blank page:

What am I afraid someone will find out about me?

Spend at least ten minutes answering this question.

Spend a few more moments rereading or looking again at what you wrote or drew. Allow the realization of what you wrote to sink in to your mind, body and heart without judging or rejecting it. Allow it to simply be part of who you are—you might want to visualize God holding this fearful, hurting or hurtful part of yourself with you.

What we know when we allow God to hold this fearful part of us is that courage comes not out of our heroism but out of a sense of being loved, an awareness so rooted and alive that we can admit our vulnerabilities without shame.

Life gives us many opportunities to embrace our vulnerabilities, not so we can treasure them but so that we can release and surrender them to God's love. And find there that grace is amazing and that we are enough. When we find grace for those moments, we also receive the strength to trust that this grace will lead us forward into a future. Only then will we see the possibilities and choices that are ours to respond to the life we are given. When we face our own vulnerability, God can become strong in our weakness. This is the sort of strength in weakness that the apostle Paul claimed for himself when he was finally able to hear God say, "My grace is enough; it's all you need. My strength comes into its own in your weakness." Paul goes on to say that when he heard this, "I quit focusing on the handicap and began appreciating the gift. It was a case of Christ's strength moving in on my weakness" (2 Corinthians 12:9-10 *The Message*).

Prayer Practice: Surrender Prayer

Acknowledging our vulnerabilities is only the first step. The second step is to surrender these fears, and even what feels wrong or off-center, to God. The ultimate truth is that you cannot save yourself; you cannot be the judge of yourself or anyone else. Such a role needs to be surrendered by your ego to God.

The prayer practice that will help you to do this is very simple, but not easy. It is called Welcoming Prayer in the spirit of providing hospitality, even welcome, for the feelings or emotions that we hide. This practice provides a place to admit the dark thoughts that sometimes live on in our souls long after our outer selves deny their existence. But I prefer to call this Surrender Prayer, because ultimately we are embracing those feelings and thoughts so that we can surrender them to God. Nevertheless, the first step is to welcome and receive, because we cannot give away what we are not yet aware of holding. Surrender Prayer can be a way of emptying ourselves as we come into God's presence. It can also be a prayer that we recall as those complicated and difficult feelings arise.

Surrender Prayer

Focus. Simply be with what you are feeling and thinking right now; welcome everything that you are holding in your body, heart and mind. Without judging it, acknowledge what is true for you and do not fight against it. Ask yourself, *Where do I feel this in my body?* Focus there, without resistance. Welcome your feelings, because they point to places where God can bring healing.

Accept and welcome. Remember that there is nothing passive about acceptance. It only establishes you in reality, in what is already true. This is an inner surrender to what you feel or think and says nothing about the situation that may have caused the emotion or feeling.

Let go and surrender. When you have fully embraced and accepted where you are, and only then, offer these thoughts, these feelings, these emotions to God. First, let go of any inner desire to change this feeling, this thought. Then say, "God, I give you this feeling, this thought. I surrender this to your work in my life." Do not move to this step too early; the heart of the welcoming prayer is in the first two steps. If another emotion or feeling rises up in you, just begin again with the first step.

Mary Mrozowski, the creator of Welcoming Prayer, always included these affirmations with the third step:

I let go of my desire for security and survival.
I let go of my desire for esteem and affection.
I let go of my desire for power and control.
I let go of my desire to change the situation.[1]

Choosing Faith

Our first inclination when we face these vulnerable, even threatening times is to resist them in some way, blocking out their danger with blame toward ourselves or others, hiding behind rationalizations or even shame-filled denials. But when we resist or block these times, we also block out an invitation to find a new orientation toward our life. Facing and accepting does not involve saying yes to the circumstances that caused our vulnerability, any more than I would have chosen the near-death of my child. But it is an invitation to fully engage life as it now is with us.

Living out of our vulnerability is not a resignation that simply settles, giving up on the outside while living in total rebellion within. But instead it says yes to life with our whole selves, even to the unpleasant and unasked-for realities of what is.

Life is the river in which we flow, and in surrender we simply acknowledge that we are capable neither of making it move nor of blocking or reversing its flow. We have only two choices—to go with the flow or to resist it. . . . Surrender invites us to a radical but always freeing posture of non-resistance to reality. It heals our relationship with life and begins to allow life to flow through rather than around or over us. It unifies our interior and outer worlds and allows us to discover new levels of openness to and intimacy with others.[2]

When life itself is the enemy, our willingness turns to willfulness, our determination into defiance. We stubbornly refuse to let go of control, even when that control is illusory.

None of this would make any sense if our surrender were not a surrender to love—a surrendering into God's relentless love for us. Often surrendering even to love can feel weak and ineffective in a culture that prizes self-mastery and control. Equally often, talk about surrender can feed our sense of self-rejection or shame, our sense of not being enough or not measuring up. Then the only viable option when we face personal weakness and brokenness is to deny its presence or become self-abusive or project it out toward those we love. It is just not safe to surrender unless that surrender is to God's transcending love. Only love invites us into an intimacy that allows surrender even of those parts of us that feel most shattered and broken. This surrender is not about being put down but about being brought close in a way that invites love's transformation. God's love frees us from being victims of our personality or our past—or our culture, sometimes even our church culture.

> Surrender is integral to Christian spirituality because, properly understood, Christian spirituality is a path of descent, not ascent. . . . It is a spirituality of following Jesus on a journey of dying to our false self so that we might

discover our true and larger identity in Christ. Self-emptying is what leads him out—returning him to the realm of dominion and glory. . . . In order to truly find our life we must first lose it (Matthew 16:24-25). And so in surrender we give up that which we think we already have, only to discover that for which we most deeply long.[3]

My own reaction to vulnerability was to fall into an abyss of self-pity followed closely by self-blame. There was nothing noble in my personal self-abnegation. As the nurse rightfully pointed out, it separated me from fulfilling my responsibilities to my son. It blocked the unfolding of my continuing life with Jesse himself. Surrendering my guilt and self-blame freed me to see him not out of fear but out of my mother-love. My attention was then not on myself but back on my child. But it also freed me to receive grace for the moment, in that difficult time when I was filled with self-condemnation. Jesus talks about receiving life through embracing suffering, even his own suffering and death, when he tells his disciples:

> Anyone who intends to come with me has to let me lead. You're not in the driver's seat; *I* am. Don't run from suffering; embrace it. Follow me and I'll show you how. Self-help is no help at all. Self-sacrifice is the way, my way, to finding yourself, your true self. What kind of deal is it to get everything you want but lose yourself? What could you ever trade your soul for? (Matthew 16:24-25 *The Message*)

The disciples did not want to hear these words. I often find myself resistant to them as well.

When Nicholas Wolterstorff's son Eric died in a mountain-climbing accident, Wolterstorff struggled and questioned God about this tragedy that would forever change his life. "Will my eyes adjust to this darkness? Will I find you in the dark—not in streaks of light which remain, but in the darkness? . . . Are there songs for singing when the light has gone dim? Or in the dark, is it best to wait in silence?"[4]

The comfort Wolterstorff found was not in "overcoming" the death of his son, as we are often encouraged to attempt, even in Christian circles, nor was it in denying the brutal loss that he had suffered. Instead he found his only comfort in lamenting his son's death in the context of his faith in God. What he found was that "lament and trust are in tension like the wood and string of the bow."[5]

Like Job's wife, one friend suggested that perhaps in the face of such unanswerable suffering and loss it might be best for him simply to give up on God. Wouldn't he be better off to acknowledge that the world is rotten and we are just pawns of feckless fate?

But Wolterstorff insists on holding on to his faith in a loving God, because he is compelled like the lamenting psalmists to pour out his grief and anger *with* God and not apart from God.

> Faith is a footbridge that you don't know will hold you up over the chasm until you're forced to walk out onto it. I'm standing there now, over the chasm. I inspect the bridge. Am I deluded in believing that in God the question shouted out by the wounds of the world has its answer? . . . I cannot dispel the sense of conducting my inspection in the presence of the Creating/Resurrecting One.[6]

What this horrific death allows him to glimpse is the suffering of God with him. It allows him to claim in a new way the Redeeming One who said, "Blessed are those who mourn, for they shall be comforted." Although history might be written toward the heroic life, being fully alive in Christ will mean mourning death and loss, and in that mourning experiencing the presence of the God who suffers with us, who dies with us, and still promises a third day of new life.

In his own mourning and the mourning of others, Wolterstorff glimpses the "anguish of God." And it is the God who suffers that is comforting those who mourn. "Upon joining the crowd on the bench of mourning, they hear the sobs and see the tears of God. By these they are consoled."[7] There is, says this grieving, bereft father, no love without suffering. Even Christ's rising into new life in the body did not remove the wounds of love's suffering. Nor does Wolterstorff come to sense the loss of his grief so much as a shared suffering and a love great enough to embrace even this worst of all pains. Surely Wolterstorff himself would urge us to not love less but to love more in light of God's enduring love for us and for those we love.

Embracing even the reality of death and our own vulnerable mortality may help us to recognize that life itself is a gift. Sometimes we are so afraid of feeling pain or feeling loss that we do not dare to love and keep on loving. Calling this the "betrayal of disengagement," author Brené Brown insists that this fear means that "we are never fully in; there is no raw engagement."[8] Being "fully in" will mean that we are fully alive with our imperfections, our vulnerabilities, our losses and even our failures and mortality. But it will also mean we are fully alive with our gifts, our enthusiasm, our possibilities and our joy. Grace allows for failure, but it also fosters joyful living. Vulnerability lived is not weakness but actually the basis for a resilience that can face suffering and even tragedy with equanimity.

In a class on Christian character we talked about the nature of Christian joy. One student insisted that there could be no real joy without its partner, sorrow. If we intend to experience joy, we needed to commit ourselves so completely to life that we are willing to experience sorrow when it comes. It is often in the places of our greatest vulnerability, our most difficult experiences, that we feel helpless, even hopeless of experiencing the depth of God's presence in the river of suffering that we are now living.

This is the truth that Henri Nouwen affirms as well when he encourages us to live in the light of Ecclesiastes 3:4 and acknowledge that there is a "time to weep, and a time to laugh; a time to mourn, and a time to dance," and they are not separate from one another.

What I want to tell you is that these times are connected. Mourning and dancing are part of the same movement of grace. Somehow, in the mist of your tears, a gift of life is given. Somehow, in the midst of your mourning, the first steps of the dance take place. The cries that well up from your losses belong to your song of praise. Those who cannot grieve cannot be joyful. Those who have not been sad cannot be glad. Quite often, right in the midst of your crying, your smile comes through your tears. And while you are mourning, you already are working on the choreography of your dance. Your tears of grief have softened your spirit and open up the possibility to say "thanks." You can claim your unique journey as God's way to mold your heart and bring you joy.[9]

At times, however, I am guilty of "foreboding joy."[10] When I forebode joy I can't enjoy what I have because I am too anxious that it will end. I think that I need to prepare for the worst instead of receiving the good that is here with me. But by constructing my own worst-case scenario, I pretend a kind of control over future events that I do not have. Worst of all, my attempts not to be blind-sided by hurt actually blind me to the good immediately with me. And they make it impossible to experience joy fully. If I long for joy, I will need to embrace the vulnerability that comes with it. And so will you.

Perhaps joy itself is the greatest vulnerability of all, because in joy we give our very selves over to the gift of faith in a future that we cannot control. It pierces us at those moments when we love or care so deeply that it creates an ache within. Perhaps this is what Jesus himself felt for the disciples during those final moments before his death, those moments when he instructed them and prayed to his Father. In Christ there was a union of joy with sorrow, love in the full knowledge of grief, denial and death.

Still, shortly before his death, Jesus reassures the disciples that they will find their sorrow turned to joy. "Very truly, I tell you, you will . . . have pain, but your pain will turn into joy. When a woman is in labor, she has pain, because her hour has come. But when her child is born, she no longer remembers the anguish because of the joy of having brought a human being into the world. So you have pain now; but I will see you again, and your hearts will rejoice, and no one will take your joy from you" (John 16:20-22). When he prays for the disciples, he asks that "they may have my joy made complete in themselves" (John 17:13).

When I live with vulnerability, I live a life of fullness rather than live a life of scarcity. I move from a life of not having enough or being enough to not only finding my true self but having Christ's joy completed in me. Joy and gratitude link our limited selves to God's transcendent presence in both good times and difficult times.

Living in Faith by Embracing Vulnerability

Listening to my life story. Was there a time when you felt vulnerable because of what you did not know, or did not understand, or because your personal limitations were exposed in some other way? What did that feel like? What was your response at the time? How do you feel about this response now? **Listening to the biblical story.** In 2 Corinthians 12:8-10, the apostle Paul speaks about his own vulnerability as a "thorn" but then insists that God's "power is made perfect in weakness." How might that happen in you? How do you understand the phrase "whenever I am weak, then I am strong"?

Listening to faith's continuing story. How does embracing your life with all its joys and sorrows, vulnerabilities and weaknesses, faithfulness and inconsistencies, make you stronger and also better able to be available for others?

Further Reading

Benner, David. *Soulful Spirituality: Becoming Fully Alive and Deeply Human*, pp. 133-66. Grand Rapids: Brazos: 2011.

"Brené Brown: How Vulnerability Holds the Key to Emotional Intimacy." Interview by Karen Bouris. *Spirituality and Health*, November-December 2012.

6

Living with Integrity

Sustaining a Life of Commitment

*T*hat Sunday morning the church community prayed and laid hands on the heads of two women. I was one of those being blessed; Vannette Thorsell was the other. I was being sent into my ordination as a minister of God's Word and the sacraments of Christian faith. Vannette was being sent back to the place where she had served as a missionary for over forty years.

I thought I knew what ordination might mean for me, but I was mostly wrong. For this journey that I publicly claimed to have chosen claimed me as well, and I was given even more than I had chosen, to my surprise and delight as well as my dismay and frustration. Vannette, too, was sure she knew where she was going and what she was sent to do as a seventy-something missionary returning to then Zaire, now the Republic of Congo. (We were never sure of her exact age, this being Vannette's single area of secret vanity.) But her life work had a surprise ending of its own as well.

Vannette was a plainspoken woman who was not afraid to

speak her mind, often staying after the weekly Bible study to offer pastoral advice to my husband, whom she considered her "young" pastor. She found me, a woman in the pulpit, to be a bit beyond the pale of advice altogether, though she did tell me she did not approve of the whole idea of women's ordination. Nevertheless, when my third child was born it was Vannette who came to my home to care for my two older children, who were both preschoolers. And it was Vannette who returned to my home two weeks later when that same third child lay in a crib in the intensive care unit at Oakland Children's Hospital and I remained at his side to nurse and to pray.

During the years of retirement at her sending church, Berkeley Covenant Church, Vannette chafed at all the changes that had come not only to her church but to the Berkeley community as well. She had, after all, not been there for the free speech movement of the 1960s or the antiwar protest culture. Its radical language dressed in denim and Birkenstock sandals affected neither her lifestyle nor her clothing choices. And she was even less aware of the comfortable computer-driven culture of the 1990s. She might have rejected it all except for the opportunity that email offered for her to stay in touch with African friends even when she was exiled to Berkeley, California.

In the congregational prayer times at Berkeley Covenant Church, Vannette read long letters from African brothers and sisters with unpronounceable, consonant-filled names who lived in circumstances and locations that we could not even imagine from the comfort of our California pews. But as we struggled to listen, just reading those letters aloud made Vannette's voice grow stronger and even more animated. She saw a whole world invisible to the rest of us, filled with vibrant colors, deep faith and unimaginable suffering.

So it was not surprising that Vannette had chosen to remain

as long as possible in her adopted home while it went from Congo to Zaire during years of unending turbulence, political repression and remarkable growth in the indigenous church. Only a sharp increase in local violence and the requirements of retirement had finally made her leave.

Six months after Vanette left with her community's blessing to return to her Africa on a short-term assignment, we received word that an intestinal obstruction proved too tenacious even for the skillful hands of the surgeon at the hospital in Karawa. The surgeon, who had grown up with Vannette as his spiritual mother, now closed her eyes, pulled the white sheet up over her face and wept.

Though the funeral in Congo was held the following day, it would be a month before there would be a memorial service for Vannette at Berkeley Covenant Church. During the time of remembering, we told stories about Vannette's determined, outspoken presence among us, and her African companion in her Berkeley home, a loud, cackling parrot that spoke an occasional word with screaming shrillness.

And then we watched the video of Vannette Thorsell's funeral in Congo. We watched as her casket was carried for miles in the sun's fierce heat by Congolese pallbearers to her burial site. And all along the sides of the road were hundreds—no, thousands—of people dressed in white, waving white handkerchiefs and scarves, weeping and crying and calling out in colonial French, with the accent of their native Lingala dialect, "Madame Vannette! Madame Vannette!"

When the long procession arrived at her burial site, the video camera zoomed into the grave itself, and there was an audible gasp from the missionaries in the congregation when we saw the grave. Though Vannette had died only the day before this burial, the grave itself was huge. It seemed the size of a foundation for a small home. Carved into its side were earthen steps that were both wide and deep. To this low spot of highest honor Madame Vannette was carried with majestic grace. It was here that she found her earthly home, even as Vannette herself was claiming her heavenly home.

As I watched the video, I understood that while Vannette lived with us in Berkeley, I never really knew her at all. But here in her home, where she had educated an entire generation of men and women who now provided the foundation for community and indigenous church leadership, not only was she known but she would never die. Here they called out her name in French and she answered them in French, in Lingala and in her own plainspoken English as well. Suddenly her spirit leaped from her spacious grave, more alive now than I had ever known her to be, visible now in a way she had never been to me before her death.

Vannette's is a story of a life lived with integrity, purpose and conviction. It is also the story of my near-total inability to see her for who she truly was until I saw her through the eyes of those Congolese mourners. Until I saw how deep the grave was, I didn't realize how my own perception of Vannette captured only the surface of who she was, missing the depth of her commitment to her vocation.

Whether they are recognized or not, people of integrity are people who are living out their vocation in the world. These Christ-followers are ordinary people, like Vannette herself, finding their desire aligned with God's desire and living this out. We see in them truthfulness and consistency, a willingness to live out the values that they claim to hold in a way that is both sacrificial and life-giving.

But Vannette also needs to be seen in the confusion and struggle she felt about living in California, and not just in the

Congo, just as Mother Teresa needs to be understood in her struggle with God's silence as she lived a life of integrity among the dying in India. Their gift to us is not godly perfection, unattainable to us, that engenders an inspiring story. Rather, their gift is utter tenacity, steadfastness, in holding on to their particular commitment and calling, even when circumstances seemed impossible or God himself seemed distant. Their goodness lies precisely in their willingness to face their own fallible, sometimes confused, even wrongheaded selves, embracing it all while letting the life of Christ rise through the ashes and glory of their humanity.

The biblical writer of Hebrews instructs us to "lay aside every weight and the sin that clings so closely, and let us run with perseverance the race that is set before us" (Hebrews 12:1). We might picture lithe young bodies in top physical shape as inspiration for a muscular Christianity striving to beat competitors to prove God's worth. But this sentence begins with the words "Therefore, since we are surrounded by so great a cloud of witnesses" and ends with Jesus' own victory that came by way of the cross (12:1-2). The witnesses who surround us are not the young and strong but the imperfect who struggled to find their way, those who wondered and wandered believing in a completion in Christ that they were not able to see or sometimes even understand. These saints and witnesses bear the burden of their sense of personal incompleteness without trying to fill the void with anything other than God.

The subtle shift that takes place as trust becomes habit and habit becomes life is that instead of having Jesus as part of our lives, we live our part as his life in the world. Instead of living *for* Jesus we live *with* Jesus, making his life our life. The inspi-

ration for such a life in Christ is not so much the running of a
race as an emptying of self.

> Let the same mind be in you that was in Christ Jesus,
>   who, though he was in the form of God,
>   did not regard equality with God
>   as something to be exploited,
>   but emptied himself,
>   taking the form of a slave,
>   being born in human likeness.
> And being found in human form,
>   he humbled himself
>   and became obedient to the point of death—
>   even death on a cross. (Philippians 2:5-8)

But here is where the paradox deepens, because in this emptying is also a finding of a true self. As we face the reality of what
we are, but also what we are not, there is no threat to our per-
sonhood, only an embrace of all that is. We've faced the brick
wall of our own will or ego, whether it hides in shame or over-
reaches in pride. We've tried to scale this wall with character
improvements, psychological insights, even spiritual understanding or practices, only to find that God's love alone can carry
us through. And even that love might be experienced as presence
only after a long dark time of absence and loss.

Most of us have experienced the frustration of the willing-doing
gap in our lives. This is the gap between what we hope or aspire
to as Christ-followers and our actual practices, thoughts and
actions.[1] The gap is often a frustration for those of us who hope
to live the life of Jesus in our own lives. Efforts to fill the willing-
doing gap with more knowledge or understanding, more experi-

ences or good works, or even more prayer and spiritual practice are often futile. Our willpower feels not powerful but empty. Even our strongly held beliefs often do not result in clearly observable changes in our nature. The discrepancies and distractions continue as our disappointment grows.

Until we finally allow God to love us not only in our doing or in our willing but—most of all—in the gap that we're unable to cross despite our best efforts.

Often this means letting God's love and forgiveness soak deeply enough in us to permeate even those parts of us that we call "false" or "shadow" selves. These selves, who thrive in the gap between our willing and doing, have their own stories to tell if only we would listen to them with love. If only we would let God embrace us in our humanness.

When we are no longer defending ourselves, we are free to love others and God out of awareness, forgiveness and acceptance. We can care honestly about others and their best interests and begin to put their needs above our own, not out of low self-esteem but out of overflowing love. We are able to laugh at ourselves and our foibles without self-deprecation but with acceptance. We offer not our effort in this acceptance but our consent to be fully loved by God as we are, not as we wish ourselves to be or as others might want to see us. "Only by opening ourselves in this way to our own frailty and finitude might we have a chance for an authentic life. Only by being hauled through hell might we have a chance of rising again. It is this that the evil cannot accept. They want to deny our frailty and negativity, not embrace it."[2]

The irony is that it is just this finitude, this fragility, that brings true goodness its undeniable beauty. The light that shines in those who live with integrity is not manufactured light, but appears as they embrace their own darkness—even their death—so that life can be seen in the Light of Christ.

> But we have this treasure in clay jars, so that it may be
> made clear that this extraordinary power belongs to God
> and does not come from us. We are afflicted in every way,
> but not crushed; perplexed, but not driven to despair; per-
> secuted, but not forsaken; struck down, but not destroyed;
> always carrying in the body the death of Jesus, so that the
> life of Jesus may also be made visible in our bodies. For
> while we live, we are always being given up to death for
> Jesus' sake, so that the life of Jesus may be made visible in
> our mortal flesh. (2 Corinthians 4:7-11)

Such heartbreakingly beautiful integrity is as difficult for us to
grasp as it was for the Corinthian church looking for a super-
apostle and finding instead the apostle Paul, whom they felt to
be weak, even a failure.

The Japanese speak of the beauty of a teapot made even more
beautiful by a crack that emerges over time as *wabi sabi*. This is
beauty of the imperfect—an artfully mended silk garment, a
slight dip in the edge of an exquisite vessel, the weathering of a
wood table with age and use. In each case the integrity is not one
of perfection but the integrity of what is true. So too it is not
striving for perfection or moral mastery or even seeking God's
approval for themselves that marks people of integrity. Instead
they are most like the surprised sheep who find themselves at
the right hand of the Good Shepherd in Matthew 25, wondering
when they gave the Son of Man food and drink and clothing or
cared for him or visited him in prison. They are not preoccupied
with their own good works. But what they experience is that the
"integrity between their beliefs and practices, though inevitably
flawed, seems to be grounded in a deep receptivity to God's mys-
terious presence."[3]

Taking a Closer Look: Participating with Christ

It is easy for us to think of life in Christ as an ascent, because we climb up from the bottom or climb the ladder of success, but life in Christ is really a *descent* into a fuller life as we participate in the life of God in the world. There is a Taizé prayer that is sung repeatedly as a chant: "The will of your love, the will of your love, be done on earth as it is in heaven." When we live with integrity, this prayer is our yes to God. It inevitably seems to involve attending to suffering, noticing pain and responding in love. "Attending to the suffering of others is not the work of self-seeking, even spiritual self-seeking. Nor is attending to suffering a matter of living up to the demands of an idealized compassionate self. Attending to suffering is simply seeing what we see when our eyes are not closed, averted or glazed over."[4]

But there is also the joy of finding the treasure hidden in the field, the pearl of great price, the joy found in the beatitude blessings promised to those who mourn and struggle. Attending to suffering invites us into this way of seeing like the father who watches every day for his child to return, while holding the pain of his beloved child's absence.

Yet even this way of seeing comes from a relaxed awareness of knowing one is loved, of knowing that while we join in God's struggle in the world, the work itself is God's ongoing work of love. We aren't striving for perfection or mastery or even completion of some ministry task, but simply to participate with Christ's own ministry, to be at the center of God's love for the world.

Where are you being invited to participate with God in the world? Sometimes these moments come up unexpectedly, when our view of the "other" is shaken by our long-held assumptions and our way of seeing is challenged, our circle of care expanded to include an enemy, outsider or stranger. This is the yes to God with our intention to follow God's path in a way that often goes unnoticed. "To say yes to doing good and then be ignored, to say yes to doing right and then be misunderstood and criticized, to say yes to being loving and then to be vilified and even crucified—this is the territory into which we will all someday be invited."[5]

Where are you being invited to say yes, even if previously you might have said no? Where is God's intention directing your intention?

Prayer Practice: Abiding Prayer

"Abide in me as I abide in you. Just as the branch cannot bear fruit by itself unless it abides in the vine, neither can you unless you abide in me" (John 15:4). When our lives are rooted in God, there is the abiding presence of Christ both within and without. Then the opening to God in our lives happens organically, not by what we do but simply by being in Christ. "I am the vine, you are the branches. Those who abide in me and I in them bear much fruit, because apart from me you can do nothing" (15:5).

Abiding prayer can be prayed in a number of ways—with an image or a prayer word or the Jesus Prayer, "Lord Jesus Christ, have mercy on me, a sinner." But in the end they are all essentially wordless prayers of simply sitting or standing or walking in the Presence. This prayer lives in the sense that you are loved, that God listens as you listen, that there is life flowing from you to God and back again. It isn't dependent on your work or insight, your experience of God or your knowledge of the Holy— it just is.

Just as the closer look began with a relaxed, nonanxious heart, so the time of abiding prayer begins with relaxed attention. The words of the Jesus Prayer, say the Orthodox teachers, simply say the truth of who Jesus is and what our own need and reality is at every moment.[6] There is no threat now in saying that I am a sinner or that I depend on the mercy of Lord for daily life. You can pray this prayer in the rhythm of your breath, while sitting at prayer or sorting the laundry or exercising at the gym. You can drop words of the prayer, but the essential word is the name of Jesus, keeping your life centered in Jesus Christ, the True Vine. This prayer is a prayer of sustainability, acknowledging that without this daily connection there is no life. It is also a prayer of consent, allowing God to be the yes at the center of your life, allowing the flow of that Life into your life.

Perhaps even this short prayer feels cumbersome and un- wieldy to sustain during our busy life. Then simply choose an- other word—Abba or Presence or God or Father or Mother or Vine or Friend or Creator—and let it be a return to the sus- taining relationship of love. You can return to the simplest prayer as you sense the Presence as close as your own breath; you are breathing in and out, held in the Spirit indwelling us and giving us life. The silence here is a silence not of distance but oneness. It is a silence not of emptiness but of an enduring relationship of love where there is infinite welcome.

The whole point of the practice is for prayer to permeate your life, so that you might sense an awareness of God in everyone and everything, even when your life is filled with noise and distractions. As you regularly and intentionally pray in this way, you will discover that "God is already present in the hidden depths of the present moment; it is just because we were skimming along across the surface of what is happening that we were unable to know and rest in that presence."[7]

Choosing Faith

When Benedict of Nursia decided to found a monastic order, he wrote what came to be called the *Rule of St. Benedict,* a guide for life together that would sustain a community committed to God and to creating an atmosphere of welcome and hospitality for one another and for the world. In order to preserve a setting of peace and holiness, the Benedictines make three promises when they join the order: to live their lives in stability, obedience and *conversio*. These three promises ground all that they do and sustain their lives of work and sacred reading and prayer. They are the heart of their integrity as a community and their participation with God. They offer a pathway of integrity with God that might be available to nonmonastics like you and me as well—giving our own work and prayer and sacred reading vocational integrity.

Stability in the Benedictine understanding is stability of place: every nun or monk pledges to remain permanently rooted in the monastery where he or she lives. But the outer stability is meant to foster an inner stability of heart to persevere in one's calling over the days and months and years. Contravening any romantic notions we might have of monastic life, this vow of stability of place and heart means consenting to let this monastery, these less-than-perfect fellow monastics and the abbot, spiritually form who you are in Christ. This commitment to stability is lived out in the commitment to everyday work that structures Benedictines' lives as much as their prayer.

While visiting a Benedictine convent, I was invited as easily into the work of candy-making as into prayer. Though I proved an abysmal failure at adding the curlicue to the tops of the chocolate caramels, the sisters found a place for me addressing boxes and filling orders. Still wearing scarves, hairnets and aprons, the sisters and I paused for prayer during the busy workday, not as a break for holiness but to remind all of us of the holiness of work itself.

You and I may not be able to commit ourselves to stability of place, but we can promise or seek to promise to live in the stability of heart that seems to characterize people of integrity. "Underneath the furious enterprise lies a center of absolute stillness, the eye of the hurricane, where they rest in the presence of God. In this silent cathedral of the heart, all on the spiritual path find at last a true stability, a home forever."[8]

Consistency in daily tasks reminds us that the spiritual life is at its core at least as much a physical as an intellectual life. Our tasks ground us in the world, just as stability of heart grounds us in God. "When old work has become meaningless and new purpose is hard to find, I recommend cleaning baseboards. . . . When I cannot tell whether that is a sleeping cat or an engorged dust ball under my bed, I know it that I have been spending too much time thinking. It is time to get down on my knees."[9] Whatever your own task is, caring for children, running a corporation, designing computer programs or housecleaning, finding purpose in high and low places supports stability of heart.

The second promise of the monastics, obedience, is supported by the sacred reading of the Benedictine community, its practice of lectio divina. Obedience comes from the Latin root *oboedire*, meaning "to listen to." The one who obeys is the one who listens. In lectio divina a passage of Scripture is read slowly, prayerfully, several times as a way of discovering what God might want to say to us. Then that word or phrase is taken into the self to be not only understood but pondered, digested and taken in until it forms and shapes a life lived with God. "Christian reading is participatory reading, receiving the words in such a way that they become interior to our lives, the rhythm and images becoming practices of prayer, acts of obedience, ways of love."[10]

For sacred reading to be obedience, it must have this participatory character of not merely hearing but truly *listening* in a way that makes meaning of what we hear and leads to a response. One day while leading a group of young mothers in the practice of lectio divina, I slowly read a story from Mark 6 where the disciples are laboring in a boat against the wind. Seeing them, Jesus comes to them on the water, but they are terrified. One of the women said that the third time I read it, she found herself on a "rabbit trail" into her own life as a mother of three young children and felt how hard she was rowing, how often it felt as if she was just pushing against the winds of clutter and demands. Then she wondered aloud, "Perhaps Jesus is as near as he was to the disciples, and I'm inclined to discount his presence as unreal and push on in my own strength. Maybe I need to find another way." This simple example illustrates not a rabbit trail but the heart of the matter. Listening that is obedience hears in the context of one's life, makes meaning and begins to articulate a response. It is listening for the One who listens to us.

That connection and companionship lead to the *conversio* that is the third promise monastics make as they take their vows. The more familiar English word *conversion* might mean for you a dramatic change or shift in direction toward a life with Christ. But *conversio* is a lifelong turning toward the transformative life in Christ. Thomas Merton spoke of *conversio* as an essential aspect of the monastic life near the end of his own life.

> When you stop and think a little bit about St. Benedict's concept of *conversatio morum,* that most mysterious of our vows which is actually the most essential I believe, it can be interpreted as a commitment to total inner transformation of one sort or another—a commitment to become a completely new man. It seems to me that that could be regarded as the end of monastic life, and that no matter where one attempts to do this, that remains the essential thing.[11]

This is not a sudden change in identity but the full realization of one's identity in Christ, one's life in God. In monastic life this *conversio* is supported by the Divine Office, the hymns, prayers and psalms that are prayed seven times a day. St. Benedict himself referred to this daily cycle of prayer as the *opus Dei,* the work of God. That work is both the prayer that the monastics pray and the work of God in the life of each of those who pray. In lectio divina, holy listening connects us to the One who listens; in the Divine Office, the monastics witness to the One who is our Witness, the One who sees.

At the heart of this prayer is another turning, one that can be identified as well in lives lived with integrity in Christ. It is a natural turning away from the duality of self and God to integration: union of self in God. This produces the transparency through which God's love shines through us as God's agenda becomes increasingly our agenda. "As we journey deeper and deeper into God, the me-in-God and the God-in-me become more and more inextricably intertwined. . . . We could even say this goal is a fulfillment of our humanity by restoring our spiritual alignment with God."[12] Yet even in this transformation we remain no less human and God remains God. One could even say that this transformation is meant to make us fully human and to understand God as totally Other. And the reality of God remains beyond all of our ideas or concepts or pictures.

A poem by George Herbert describes both the adoration and the invitation that lies at the center of this self-in-God and God-in-self that is the integrity of conversion. What a life of integrity offers is a heart of joyful love that can never be taken away by life's circumstances, or even death itself.

The Call
Come, my Way, my Truth, my Life:
Such a Way, as gives us breath:
Such a Truth, as ends all strife:
Such a Life, as killeth death.

Come, my Light, my Feast, my Strength:
Such a Light, as shows a feast:
Such a Feast, as mends in length:
Such a Strength, as makes his guest.

Come my Joy, my Love, my Heart:
Such a Joy, as none can move:
Such a Love, as none can part:
Such a Heart, as joys in love.[13]

Living in Faith by Living with Integrity

Listening to my life story. Who is the person who comes to your mind and heart as you think of a person of integrity? What do you see in this person that identifies her or him as a person of integrity? How have you incorporated these virtues in your own life, or how might you?

Listening to the biblical story. In Philippians 2:5-11 the writer implies that we can, in fact, have the "mind of Christ." How is the description of Christ's emptying and exaltation related to integrity and having the "mind of Christ"?

Listening to faith's continuing story. How does your identity in Christ lead to a transparency that allows others to see Christ in you?

Further Reading

Kang, Joshua Choonmin. *Deep-Rooted in Christ: The Way of Transformation.* Downers Grove, IL: InterVarsity Press, 2007.

Willard, Dallas. "Children of Light and the Light of the World." In *Renovation of the Heart: Putting on the Character of Christ,* pp. 217-33. Colorado Springs: NavPress, 2002.

PART THREE

Choosing Hope

7

Paying Attention

Watching for God

 W e have to arrive early to be sure to get a seat," the Native pastor tells us. But when we arrive the seats in the high school auditorium are mostly empty. The pastor, a Native Alaskan from the village of Mekoryuk, on Nunivak Island out on the Bering Sea, sits down only long enough to place his parka on the chair. Then, looking around to see who is there and who is coming in, he reaches out his hand and greets everyone. I quickly realize that the real reason he wanted to arrive early was so that he could greet friends and relatives from the western coast of Alaska and the villages along the Yukon as well. The Musicale is a yearly singspiration held over a week of evenings during Anchorage's long winter. Native musical groups and soloists come from all over western Alaska and as far north as Barrow, above the Arctic Circle.

The day before I'd flown in on Alaska Air from Chicago with the distinct sense of arriving in an entirely different place. This is my first visit to Alaska, but I am more than a tourist because

I know I may well be visiting my new home. My husband is a candidate for a pastoral position in Anchorage; we are deciding whether we would consider moving here, as the church decides whether or not to invite us. Just as Dorothy in *The Wizard of Oz* had reminded herself, "You're not in Kansas anymore," I know that I am no longer in Chicago. My disorientation only increases when I realize that no one else seems to be really from Anchorage, either. The program for the evening carefully states where each soloist and singing group is from and then where it is *really* from. Singers living in Anchorage are really from Scammon Bay and Shaktoolik and White Mountain, just as the pastor lives in Anchorage but is really from Mekoryuk. Already I am experiencing the geographical precision of Alaskans, whose first question is "Where are you from?" And the necessary corollary is "Where are you really from?" All us have arrived here but are really from another place, another home. Anchorage itself is often not a place you *come from* but one you *come to*. Some Native Alaskans come here for health care, others come for jobs, but everyone comes to Anchorage to shop at Costco.

Behind the stage I see a painted mural of mountains, black spruce trees, a log cabin and a fish camp, placing us all in rural Native Alaska, despite the auditorium's location in Anchorage. In front of the mural are four guitarists, two accordionists and a fiddle player or two. As the crowd gathers the gospel band of Native musicians plays together. There seems to be no set list of songs to be followed but a leader who plays opening chords as the others lean in to catch what the melody might be. Satisfied that they know the song, they then lean back in their chairs and join in. As each subsequent person or musical group gets up to sing and play, there is a similar leaning in by the musicians to catch the song and then leaning back as they hold on to it.

When the musical groups get up to perform their two or three songs, it often seems as if the crowd, like the Native pastor, is more intent on visiting than on listening. But as a stranger in this crowd of family and friends, I am riveted by the performers on the stage—a mix of old and young people, sometimes with words of testimony to share as well as a song. The musical style is definitely country-western gospel, always with the twang of an electric guitar bridge between two of the verses. But the musical offerings themselves seem to be less about excellence or polished performance than about the sincerity and authenticity of the singers' life in Christ. In fact, sometimes the musical offerings can be so out of tune as to seem purposely dissonant. But no one can miss the plaintive, simple, almost naked belief that emanates from each person on the stage.

Most wear the traditional kuspuks over their jeans and running shoes, with the occasional pair of mukluks. The kuspuk is made of cotton fabric in a style that resembles a parka without the warm lining, and with the hood and pocket trimmed with ribbon or rickrack edging. A woman's kuspuk is made of a fabric printed with small flowers or another natural design, often with a deep ruffle that falls anywhere from the knee to midthigh. The men's kuspuk is in a solid-colored fabric with decorated hood and pockets, but no ruffle, of course. Mukluks are traditional sealskin boots trimmed with caribou fur and decorated with beadwork.

The chatting among the audience continues as the first groups finish singing and more of the audience arrives. Then a husband comes onto the stage pushing his wife in a wheelchair, and the crowd turns forward and becomes quiet. The couple sings a duet of the translated song "Does Jesus Care?" I know the tune and the English lyrics of this gospel song, but not these words. The Native pastor's wife leans over and whispers, "They're singing in Eskimo." Later, I will learn that the words are in Yu'pik. But I can hear in her urgent whisper that listening to this song is different. I see tears welling up in her eyes, and I understand that the song is being sung in her heart language. As verse follows verse, the audience all around me is still, held in rapt attention. Still observing, I wonder how it reaches the audience as the singers begin the refrain yet again, with its strong affirmation of Jesus' tender presence: "Oh yes, he cares, I know he cares, / his heart is touched with my grief. / When the days are weary, the long nights dreary, / I know my Savior cares."

But then I drop down into the song and hear it not as someone listening to others and watching those around me. Suddenly I am the weary one who longs more than anything to simply believe for myself that I have a Savior who cares. I feel a catch in my throat as I sing along in my own heart language those words of comfort when the chorus is repeated once more in English. Soon the couple shuffles off the stage with a simple "Quyana, Jesus" (thank you, Jesus), and the moment has passed. But it has not ended, because the song echoes within my heart, finding its resonant depths and settling within my soul.

Looking back, I've wondered whether it was just this soul weariness that finally led me to move to Anchorage. Where I lived before, everyone I knew boasted about how busy they were—almost as if busyness itself were a badge of importance or at least recognition. Making appointments with others meant looking at weeks ahead in an appointment calendar to find a mutually agreeable time. But there was something more—it seemed that the pace itself increased my sense of worry and anxiety about what I was doing and how others were seeing me. The truth was I was exhausted with myself, my outlook and my self-centered concerns when I agreed to move to Alaska. Still, actually moving here was more than a bit scary.

As a child I played the game of skipping a stone across the surface of the lake. In my recent life I had played that game as an adult, skipping stones along the surface of my life and boasting about how many skips I could make. Here in Alaska that stone dropped down and found its depth. Letting go of a position and an office, even a telephone number, felt like a larger letting go than I had expected. Alaska's sense of the "big, wide open" was intimidating. I avoided looking at a map, not wanting to see the vast distance between me and the places I had left behind. Sometimes I even avoided the horizon's view out my window toward the mountains, preferring instead the contained view of a book or a movie or television show.

Eventually, I began to lift up my head, look around and pay attention to my surroundings. My times of actually being here, present to all that is in this place, slowed me down, made me stop. At the same time, I felt as if I was waking up. The light, the sky, the very "big, wide open" that I had avoided during those first months now stunned me with their uncommon, sometimes even eerie beauty. Like the moose that appear unexpectedly along the road or on the bike path, or simply walking across the little street outside my office window, these moments continue to surprise me, nearly throw me off balance, stop me in my own tracked and rutted ways. And they happen here more often than in any other place I have lived. Sometimes you have time to gaze and take it in, but other times the alpenglow of the mountains backlit by the sun setting or rising is brief and fleeting. I notice it as I'm driving at sixty miles an hour on the Seward Highway. On a good day, I'll pull off the highway to fill up not just my eyes but my being with amazement.

Author Tony Hiss describes these moments as instances of *deep travel.* "In an instant our sense of the here and now that we're part of expands exponentially, and everything around is so vivid and intensely experienced that it's like waking up when we are already awake."[1] These moments can be unexpected and surprising, taking us from unawareness into an almost transcendent awareness, as often happens with me in Alaska. Hiss contends that this way of seeing is innate in all of us, a kind of knowing that is elusive but real, and it is often our inattention that dulls this ability. Living in Alaska has deepened this kind of knowing in me and given me back that soul-expanding sense of wonder that is both childlike and the wisdom of true experience.

Deep travel demands an awareness of the moment, a lesson that I have not always been quick to learn. Shortly after I arrived in Anchorage a friend with a truck and two kayaks suggested that we go kayaking on Westchester Lagoon. We went out and had a great time, watching the birds nesting on the island and swimming all around us. The following week she offered again to take me kayaking, this time on Sand Lake. But by then my own to-do list had grown longer, and I told her I was too busy. "Well, Helen," my friend, a longtime Alaskan, warned me, "it is coming toward the end of the best time to go out." And she was right. A couple of days later a cold front with rain cheated me out of another chance to see birds and float languidly along a placid lake's surface. But then it was not the weather that cheated me but my own inattention to what mattered most.

And I've had other invitations to travel deeply, not in miles but in years. I'm part of a writing group in which we write weekly on a prompt and gather to read our writing aloud. What makes this group unique is that at sixty I am almost twenty years younger than the next youngest member. The oldest is ninety-four, followed by an accomplished poet who is eighty-nine. This too provides a view I might have missed because of my inexperience. One of the women in the group is a doctor who traveled by dogsled to see patients in the bush, off the road system; others were nurses during World War II, while another was one of the first public health nurses among the Natives in western Alaska. The poet came here from New York City, buying a gold claim in what is now Denali National Park. Another remembers putting up blackout curtains as a nurse in a Sussex hospital when Neville Chamberlain declared war on Hitler's Germany.

Sitting with these women weekly, hearing the way they remember details of childhood prairie landscapes, the rebuilding after the 1964 earthquake, and Alaskan travel before snow machines or four-wheelers, and with only a little plane travel, is humbling and wonderful. And it makes me think that genuine humility seems to be a prerequisite for the wonder of deep travel as well as for its outcome. Hiss writes that "being humble (the 'holy virtue' that according to Dante, acts as an antidote to pride) or at least being more forthright and honest about what you know and don't know . . . can certainly restore a far wider range of awareness."[2]

Taking a Closer Look: Dropping the Hook

Surely this type of seeing was available to me before I moved to Anchorage. However, Alaska opened my eyes by revealing a landscape that I didn't know but that seemed to know me. Even here I never would have noticed it if I had not slowed down enough to be part of the natural and human world around me.

I remember asking a colleague in Chicago, "How are you?" I asked not casually but with some genuine concern for his well-being.

He responded, "I'm pedaling as fast as I can."

Too many times I too have been moving quickly but missing out on any genuine encounter with myself or the world around me. When our pace is that driven, even those things we accomplish are done without true attention or discernment about what matters most.

The most famous Alaskan sport is not basketball or baseball or even hockey, but dog mushing. Each year the Iditarod run of around a thousand miles from Willow to Nome by as many as sixty-six dogsled teams is front-page news in Anchorage and all over the state. A dogsled typically has twelve to sixteen dogs that pull the musher and sled over fierce mountains, frozen rivers, spruce forests and snowy tundra, with high winds causing wind-chill temperatures of –100 degrees F at times. Mushers cannot add more dogs along the way and must still have at least five of the original dog team when completing the race.

The dogs are bred to run; left to themselves, they would run until their hearts burst. But a good musher takes care of the dogs carefully, giving them plenty of food and love, and forcing them to stop. Of course, getting the lead dog's attention in the middle of a ferocious winter storm is not always easy. The lead dog may not hear the musher's voice over the wind and the barking of the other dogs. So if the dog cannot hear the command to stop, the musher drops a hook into the ground to let the lead dog know it is time to stop. When the lead dog feels the pull of the hook slowing the sled, it knows to slow down the team.

At times I realize that my own life has felt as if there were a team of dogs rushing me forward. There are lots of necessary and good things in our lives that are like that team of sled dogs: work and family, community and church responsibilities that each of us could name in more detail. They are important to us, as the dogs are to the musher. They carry us over life's rough terrain and through storms of all sorts; they provide stability and direction. They are meant to help us "run with perseverance the race that is set before us, looking to Jesus the pioneer and perfecter of our faith"(Hebrews 12:1-2). As we run, we are meant to be aware of the challenge and the comfort, the patience and perseverance, the love and goodness that these dogs have given and taught us.

Spend a few moments now to simply list the ten or so people and communities and places that pull your life's sled forward and that may have even carried you over rough patches along the way. Then pay attention to the gift they are to you, giving thanks for each of these in your life. Perhaps you can recall times when you shared love and affection, times when you learned something new or reached a significant milestone. Just like those sled dogs, each one has a name and a particular role in your life story.

Now look back on the past week and ask yourself when you "dropped the hook" and stopped it all so that you and these dogs you love could rest. When even good things run out of control, without stopping to rest, then those good things fill our need for security or esteem or control or power, and we run them until their hearts wear out, or until we ourselves are completely burned out. Those good things—work and even church or family responsibilities and acts of compassion—can become addictions that prop us up to keep us going, instead of providing comfort, direction and hope. When that happens, we are no longer able to pay attention to God or the world he created for us to enjoy. We are no longer "looking to Jesus the pioneer and perfecter of our faith" but are building up our own ego. How willing are you to drop the hook so that you can really rest from it all and offer the good things in your life the nurture and rest and care that they need?

You may be struggling with addictions that are especially destructive and hurtful to you and everyone else. Alcoholism, drug addiction, sexual addictions and the cycle of abuse are not good dogs that can be tamed. These dogs are determined to lead you off course and away from your true self and God. The only answer is for you to drop the hook, and with the help of God and perhaps a sponsor, stop. This stopping may not be only to rest but to survive.

Take a step back from your life just now. Ask yourself if it feels driven and compulsive as you run the race, or if you are able to pay attention to the world around you and grow in self-awareness as you move through your life.

Prayer Practice: Sabbath

The rules of the Iditarod Race require the musher to take a mandatory twenty-four-hour stop along the way, as well as two eight-hour stops. Perhaps it is helpful to think of sabbath as a mandatory twenty-four-hour stop along each of our week-runs through life.

> Remember the sabbath day, and keep it holy. Six days you shall labor and do all your work. But the seventh day is a sabbath to the LORD your God; you shall not do any work— you, your son or your daughter, your male or female slave, your livestock or the alien resident in your towns. For in six days the LORD made heaven and earth, the sea, and all that is in them, but rested the seventh day; therefore the LORD blessed the sabbath day and consecrated it. (Exodus 20:8-11)

This commandment is part of the basic core behavior codes that God gave to the Hebrew people that were meant for their good and the good of those around them. Both the beauty and the difficulty of the traditional weekly Jewish sabbath are that it comes at sundown, whether or not you have accomplished all that you hoped, whether or not you feel ready, whether or not preparations are complete. The sun sets and sabbath begins. It is like the twenty-four-hour rest along the thousand-mile run of the Iditarod; it is a mandatory rest.

I grew up with a mandatory sabbath on Sundays in my Dutch Reformed community. We did not buy or sell anything on the sabbath (this was considered work, or causing others to work). Exceptions to the work rule were made only for the volunteer firemen, the dairy farmers who had to milk their cows and perhaps the wives and mothers still expected to prepare the Sunday dinner. I admit that as a child I didn't always experience the sabbath as a gift. Often the rules about what we were not to do felt constraining. And it sometimes seemed as if what was required of us was not a mandatory sabbath but mandatory church attendance.

So in adulthood, when my husband suggested that I might need a weekly sabbath when I was a busy mom and part-time pastor, I felt a resurgence of childish rebellion. It would have been helpful then for me to understand the Iditarod stipulation for the mandatory twenty-four-hour stop—that it may be taken at a time that is most beneficial to the dogs. As it was, I did recall the teachings of Jesus as he healed the man with a withered hand on the sabbath and helped the bent-over woman to stand tall in the synagogue. "'I desire mercy and not sacrifice.' ... For the Son of Man is lord of the sabbath" (Matthew 12:7-8). And when he was criticized for curing on the sabbath, he accused his accusers of being hypocrites for caring for their animals on the sabbath and yet pointing the finger at him. "And ought not this woman, a daughter of Abraham whom Satan bound for eighteen long years, be set free from this bondage on the sabbath day?" (Luke 13:16).

My own sabbath began not as a mandatory twenty-four-hour stop but as an eight-hour stop in my week. Late Tuesday afternoon, my husband came home so he could care for the three children. I drove away from my home, letting go of children and dinner, bath and bedtimes. My sabbath times were always the same, and I loved the ritual of each part of the evening. I began by eating fresh, wholesome food with lots of vegetables that my children did not yet appreciate. Then I went swimming and sat in the sauna at the YMCA in Berkeley, where we were living at the time. After my meal and swim, I settled into a coffeehouse with a decaf mocha and wrote in my journal. Those first journal entries were a return to my long-neglected relationship with God that had been pushed aside by the needs of my family, my church and even my marriage. The first few times I expected to be admonished for my disregard of God's love and presence, which had been there all along. But what I found instead was hospitality and welcome—always. I had to look at some hard things in my life during those evenings, but even those came to me with love and freedom.

My sabbath was a mandatory rest. If I waited longer to make sure that I finished my tasks or that my husband's dinner or entertainment choices for the children met my own requirements, I might never leave. I wouldn't drop the hook. But my husband would see me and say, "What are you still doing here?" He knew that if I set aside this time for myself, I would be better able to make healthy, life-giving choices for all the dogs in my life, including him.

It wasn't long before he, too, wondered if he could take a night for his own sabbath. I also found another evening for sabbath that began with playing cards in the late afternoon with a friend and included our whole family in the eight hours of rest, with a shared meal and a movie. With my children grown, I'm now able to take a twenty-four-hour mandatory sabbath, but I loved those eight-hour evening breaks with and without my husband, children and friend. And I miss the way they gave anticipation and joy to my whole week.

Author Wayne Mueller writes that one of the most astonishing things about sabbath is its "unflinching uselessness. Nothing will get done, not a single item will be checked off any list. Nothing of significance will be accomplished, no goal realized. It is thoroughly without measurable value."[3] I believe he is right in saying this makes many of us, including me, uncomfortable. Even my current Sunday afternoon doze, which I love, feels more than a little indolent. But perhaps we all just need to realize that it is good to stop doing and doze. Mueller says that we can become "enthralled by the trance of work" without this sabbath. When we live in this trance, we are convinced that we cannot stop or it will all fall apart. We easily go from the trance of work to the trance of consuming more and better things. Soon work and consuming holds us in their grip, with our attention riveted to a cycle of doing and having. Sabbath breaks into this cultural pattern and calls us home to ourselves and to God. Just as the musicians leaned into the song and then leaned back as they began to play the tunes, sabbath allows you to lean into your life, so that you catch the melody at its center and lean back to play it out.

So many of the best spiritual practices seem counterintuitive, and certainly sabbath is a prime example of this. We say no to all of our regular activities so that we can pay attention to all that we have missed, so we can discern more clearly the heart of the matter for our lives. It's almost as if we need to take a Sunday rest so that we can wake up to what is happening within and around us. We say no so that our yes can be yes—not halfheartedly, but a wholehearted, generous yes. It would seem that saying no to some things allows us to be alert, ready and watchful for others. This wakefulness that begins with rest is at the heart of our faith in a God who is larger than our lives and could break in at any moment. It is the alertness demanded of those who choose to pay attention.

Choosing Hope

Paul says to the Christians in Rome, "You know what time it is, how it is now the moment for you to wake from sleep. For salvation is nearer to us now than when we became believers; the night is far gone, the day is near. Let us then lay aside the works of darkness and put on the armor of light." In fact, he goes on to say, it is time to "put on the Lord Jesus Christ" (Romans 13:11-12, 14).

Expanding on these words, Quaker writer Douglas Steere believes prayer itself is about "waking up out of the dull sleep in which our life has been spent in half-intentions, half-resolutions, half-creations, half-loyalties, and becoming actively aware of the real character of that which we are and of that which we are over against." Steere calls this the "shaking off of the grave-clothes . . . a dip in acid . . . daring to read the text of the universe in the original."[4] Paying attention is a waking up into life as it truly is, not as we wish it to be or as it was somewhere in a happier past.

In Chicago it often seemed that people survived in a large metropolitan city by dividing it into smaller neighborhoods, sometimes identifying so closely with a neighborhood that the rest of the city might never be explored. But in Alaska there is always a stretching of geography and place beyond one's comprehension, always pushing the limits of the knowable. My license plate reminds me that this is the last frontier, and as in every frontier there is the longing for all that can still be explored and experienced. There is an almost palpable sense of the More that might be here if only we would put on our hiking boots and walk all the way to the edge of wherever we happen to be.

But there is more that Alaska has taught me, and that is the humility of all that I do not know. Alaskans shake their heads as they watch a tourist, terrified of meeting a bear in the wild, walk up to the moose for a close-up picture. We know that the moose is wild and unpredictable and able to kill you with one casual kick of his substantial hooves. We know more people are killed by moose each year than bears. What you don't know not only could hurt you, it could kill you, whether you are hiking on a mountain, traversing a glacier or simply trying to take a photograph of the unpredictable moose.

Humility about what you know and do not know is essential for paying attention. David James Duncan says this demands not only a strategic withdrawal from work and busyness but a "refusal to man our habitual demographic, political, or psychological trenches and defend our turf. . . . This withdrawal might be any act you can devise . . . that embodies the willingness to wait for the world to disclose itself to you rather than to disclose yourself."[5] Such willingness is at the core of humility's connection to paying attention. Mueller notes that

> the word *humility*, like the word *human*, comes from *humus*, or earth. We are most human when we do no great things. We are not so important; we are simply dust and spirit—at best loving midwives, participants in a process much larger than we. If we are quiet and listen and feel how things move, perhaps we will be wise enough to put our hands on what waits to be born, and bless it with kindness and care. But in the end, we are granted the tremendous blessing of knowing that we do very little at all by ourselves.[6]

This is also an apt description of poverty of spirit, which I believe is the core of true humility. It is being less-than so that God can have the rightful place of more-than; it is allowing creation to reveal itself rather than placing our stamp on the world. Without this perspective, we will look to establish ourselves and our significance and uniqueness by our own goals and "degenerate into a greed in spirit and in body which makes wonder, awe, full awareness, and the sheer gaze of admiration impossible."[7] The fear of God is the beginning of wisdom because it allows us to be human and gives God the space to be truly God. Seeing God for who God is offers us the sweet relief of *not* being God, of being blessedly human. When we embrace our creatureliness, the remarkable people around us will be revealed, friends and enemies alike, for who they truly are. Then creation itself can open up to the possibility of wonder and surprise and mystery.

Ultimately, this place of standing on earth, the level ground under the cross, is not only the place we are from; it is the place we are *really* from. This is the truest answer to the ubiquitous Alaska question.

Living in Hope by Watching for God

Listening to my life story. Recall a time when you were asked to "pay attention." What were the circumstances? What helped you to wake up and see or hear or feel or understand something in a way that surprised you?

Listening to the biblical story. Read Exodus 3:1-6. Why did the angel tell Moses to take off his sandals because where he stood was holy ground? Why must we sometimes take things off to receive God's presence? What would it mean for you to "remove your sandals"?

Listening to hope's continuing story. How can paying attention lead toward hope? How might you begin to live in more conscious awareness of God's presence in your relationships, your community and your world?

Further Reading

Au, Wilkie. "Walking with Mindfulness." In *The Enduring Heart: Spirituality for the Long Haul*, pp. 96-121. Mahwah, NJ: Paulist, 2000.

Ford, Leighton. *The Attentive Life: Discerning God's Presence in All Things*. Downers Grove, IL: InterVarsity Press, 2008.

8

Seeing Blessing

Living in Possibility

*T*here was not a trace of pity in his face or his tone when he looked at me and said, "What's new?"

I was not surprised to see the new pastor of our church at my bedside. But it was unusual for anyone, especially a pastor, to look directly at me during a hospital visit, and stranger still to see an open, friendly face. These required preoperative pastoral visits to my hospital bedside were usually marked by a fleeting Scripture, a childish prayer, a shared embarrassment. By then I was an angry, belligerent preadolescent who was profoundly unhappy about facing her fourth orthopedic surgery in six years, knowing there was at least one more (it turned out to be two more) in the next years. But my bad attitude or circumstances or even my age did not seem to put off this visitor or make him uncomfortable. Instead he seemed genuinely interested in me, really seeing me and not just a hospital patient on the pediatric floor. Over time, I realized that this pastor actually saw someone that I myself had not yet met.

What he saw was a girl with a significant hospital story and a lifelong limp but who was intelligent and bright. It was this pastor who introduced me to the woman who might be lurking within my angry preteen self. He prodded me to talk, to laugh and especially to think for myself. After that first real conversation in the hospital, this minister became my pastor, and then he became my friend. Through him I started to believe that God cared about what I thought, not simply whether my thinking was right or not, but my original thoughts. Because I could see that this adult, God's minister, saw beyond my obvious disability and valued my abilities.

While others brought me stuffed animals to comfort me, he brought me books to challenge me. Through these gifts I met thoughtful people of faith who introduced me to new perspectives. Clearly, there was a whole world of understanding that I had missed in my rather narrow, rule-bound Christian upbringing. While in my family and church we all chatted easily about people in our community or the Wisconsin weather, I had never before met anyone who wanted to talk about my ideas.

Several years later, this same pastor decided to give a Bible exam and told me if I passed this test I would be allowed to skip the endless youth Bible classes at the church. In exchange for this reprieve, I read the books he assigned and agreed to write a personal "research paper" comparing Simon and Garfunkel lyrics (my mid-1960s music passion) to my new Christian theological understandings. The paper was long and pretentious, showing more what I as a sixteen-year-old did not know than what I did know. But my pastor loved every word of it.

Our church community was characteristically in denial of any personal or familial problems. These were carefully hidden behind outward cultural conformity to the mores and values of the community. I myself was explicitly forbidden to speak about our family's inevitable dysfunctions and failures, most especially with the pastor. Though I did not speak with him directly about my family's troubles, I conversed with him about it all in the privacy of my mind. Even as a silent partner to my personal troubles, large and small, I could count on him to always listen with love.

During my senior year of high school, I participated in my school's forensics group, winning a first at state in original oration. It occurred to me that this gift in public speaking had some resemblance to a gift in preaching. But I dismissed as nonsense these first thoughts of becoming a minister myself. After all, I had grown up in a church where women didn't even usher people to their pew—where women were never allowed to teach men, only women and children.

But my pastor and friend instilled in me a commitment to God and a love for theology that would not go away. When I became a social worker instead of a minister, he urged me to go to seminary to "complete my graduate education." After I graduated from seminary, he was surprised, and a bit uncomfortable, to learn that I actually intended to become a minister. "Well," I said to my pastor friend, "that's what happens when you go to seminary. Perhaps it is not surprising that I became a pastor, because you were both the one who encouraged me and my model as pastor." Still he insisted that he never intended for me to follow this path, because he could not justify it within the boundaries of his strict biblical interpretation. Yet it was hard to mistake his obvious delight in celebrating our shared vocation. At the end of our conversation he gave me a big smile and an even bigger hug. Yet again, his pastoral care and unique love for me as a person won out over his stated belief regarding women in ministry.

I was never invited to share the pulpit in that church, but I never doubted that he watched me as my ministry life unfolded in Chicago and then in Berkeley, California. When I became engaged to my husband, I sought his approval as eagerly as my own father's. He drove from Wisconsin to my wedding in Chicago to give his personal blessing. But my friend and pastor's blessing to me had come much earlier, on that day when he pulled his chair up to my hospital bed on the pediatric floor, when he looked at me and truly saw me. Though the looks from my family and community members were often of pity and sadness, the look of my pastor and friend redeemed what I believed to be my damaged self.

Because my mother continued to live in the small Wisconsin community where I grew up, I continued to see my former pastor on visits even after he had retired from the church of my childhood. Those meetings were always filled with the same look of love and blessing that he had offered to me so many years earlier. One evening toward the end of his life, he was having dinner with his wife at a restaurant where my mother and I were just being seated. By then I was a minister, a wife and mother of three children. When he saw me, my pastor friend came over to greet me. A tall man, he stood behind me, placed his hands on my shoulders, leaned his long frame over me and asked, "How's the Reverend Mother?"

Taking a Closer Look: The Reflection in Our Mirrors

Most of us look at our reflections in mirrors all day long. We look at mirrors that were given to us by our parents or our teachers, our bosses and siblings, as we have carried these mirrors into our relationships, our workplaces and our faith communities. Usually the first mirror that comes to mind is the one that shows our flaws, our imperfections, even our habitual sins. The reflection we see in that mirror encourages us to mask everything that does not feel right; or to begin on a self-improvement plan to find the perfect self; or simply to give up and accept that we are defined by the things that are not right about the way we look or act, what we know or how we feel about ourselves or others.

However, each of us has been given another mirror. We received it from a loving grandmother or nurturing parent, a favorite teacher, a close friend or a pastor. When my pastor sat down at my hospital bed, he had every reason to resent having to visit me, or at the very least to pity me. But instead he offered a new mirror that gave me a picture of myself I might have missed altogether. When he offered me that view of myself, he blessed me.

Just for a moment now, lay down the first view that shows each blemish, every weakness, and pick up this mirror that shows another side of who you truly are. The look of blessing offers you a glimpse of what is and a hint of what might be. It is clear-eyed enough to see what is wrong, but it always highlights the gift that you are, the image of God that might be tarnished but is right there in plain sight in your life.

As you look at yourself in the mirror held out to you by those who love you best, what do you see? Do you see your loving nature, your sense of humor, your bright intelligence, your generosity, your gift of healing or teaching or listening? Sometimes the look of blessing reveals the more hidden fruits of the Spirit—a genuine affection for others, or an exuberance about life; a serenity of spirit or a willingness to stick with things; perhaps a sense of compassion, a conviction that a basic holiness permeates all things, loyalty to your commitments, or an ability to direct your energies wisely and not force your way in life (see Galatians 5:22-23 *The Message*).

The more we look into the mirror that magnifies our fears, our inadequacies, our unattractive features and our sin, the less likely we are to notice the look of blessing. Perhaps the critical mirror's view began as an almost casual, seemingly innocent assumption that you were the silly one, or the less pretty, not as athletic or as smart or as good as someone else. Comparison seems to be bred into the bone of each of us until we find ourselves trapped by the way we look in relation to others and not who we were created to be in Christ. When we spend our time looking to the right and the left, we ourselves end up in the center—in striving to be better than someone else, we become completely self-centered. And there is little opportunity for God to speak truth into our lives, or God's own longing that we might live into all that he has always hoped for us.

Make a list of what you see in the mirror that highlights your imperfections, your less successful side or your outright failure. Then make a second list of what you see reflected in the look of the person who loves or loved you best. As you look at the two lists, which one carries the most weight in the way you see yourself? If the first list seems to define who you are, your tendency might be to move toward guilt or shame, bitterness or discontent about yourself. You may become disillusioned with your life and feel a sense of dread rather than anticipation about the future. But when you let your life be shaped by the truth in the list of the one who knows and loves you, there is a sense of the good, and you live not in dread but in hope. This look gives you God's view into the heart of your being, your soul; it reveals the image of God rooted in you from the very beginning.

Choosing blessing for yourself can be a struggle, especially if the look of shame clings to the way that you see yourself. Shame can fill up the reflected look with its toxic presence. This shaming can deny the very image of God within us, leading us to believe that our created essence is defective. It can be a long process for those living with shame to choose to believe the look of blessing. However, if we rely on the negative mirror to look at ourselves, we will inevitably offer that same mirror to those around us. Finding the freedom to choose the mirror of love and blessing for ourselves means that we can choose to offer this mirror to others as well.

For not only do we choose the mirror we look into every day to see ourselves, we also offer our view of others to those around us. Each of us can choose to bless—or not. When we use our power to bless, we see and understand others from a different perspective. And we also help others see themselves in a new light. According to Celtic author John O'Donohue, a blessing can be surprisingly effective in improving our own eyesight. "In the light and reverence of blessing, a person or situation becomes illuminated in a completely new way. In a dead wall a new window opens, in dense darkness a path starts to glimmer, and into a broken heart healing falls like morning dew."[1]

But how do we do this, especially in a culture focused on pointing out what defects need to be fixed or what problems need to be solved, or at least on giving a word of advice to the needy parts of ourselves or others?

Prayer Practice: Choosing to See Blessing

Our usual way of looking at ourselves is to first glance in the mirror of blessing but then take a long look in the mirror that highlights flaws and creates judgment—and we do the same for others. We believe this to be helpful, since it lets the other person see where they can improve, but it actually ends up highlighting personal failures. "Helen is an insightful and, at odd moments, even a wise person, but she is often forgetful and disorganized." Now whatever insightfulness I might have is buried in my piles of forgetful disorganization. True, to be sure, but the potential and possibilities of insight and occasional wisdom are lost to me as I focus on my failure. On the other hand, if I switch those views around, I can see that though I am disorganized and often forgetful, I am insightful, and at odd moments even wise. I can accept myself for who I am in light of my gifts, not my failures. (I might even use that insight to become better organized, but don't count on it.)

I find this practice of blessing has a significant effect not only on how I see myself but also on how I see my children, my spouse and my faith community. It is not that blessing the world *makes* things and people holy. What I see instead is that "holiness is already there, embedded in the very givenness of things. . . . Because God made these beings, they share in God's own holiness, whether or not they meet your (or my) minimum requirements for a blessing."[2]

Nearly every time I teach this practice in a workshop at a class, I find that at least one person resists it, convinced that the more righteous and holy action is to hold on to judgments. But I am even more convinced that the world needs our blessing, and through us the blessing of God. And the church, as followers of Jesus, who tells us that the greatest commandment is to love, needs to choose blessing rather than cursing. If we can learn to bless ourselves and bless one another, transformation just might be possible.

Even the biblical understanding of salvation relies on an acceptance of blessing both in its personal view and in its theological vision. In his letter to the Romans, the apostle Paul insists, "The wages of sin is death, but the gift of God is eternal life" (Romans 6:23). Our salvation is seen not in light of sin but of the gift of God and eternal life itself. Peter tells a huddled group of persecuted Christians, "Once you were not a people, but now you are God's people; once you had not received mercy, but now you have received mercy." These are the ones he calls a "chosen race, a royal priesthood, a holy nation, God's own people, in order that you may proclaim the mighty acts of him who called you out of darkness into his marvelous light" (1 Peter 2:9-10).

God does not love us in spite of our humanity but in our fallible human form. And God loves the world in its own imperfect glory. When my childhood pastor chose to see me in blessing—Helen may be an angry preteenager with hip dysplasia, but she is bright and interesting—he brought to my bedside nothing less than God's look toward me. By bringing me this blessing, he also found out more about me. He knew I longed to trust that God could love me as I was in the hospital bed, that God could see the more that I might be. And he sensed, like any good pastor, that I would never get there on my own; I needed him to bless me and show me the way to God.

As Barbara Brown Taylor writes so eloquently,

> Pronouncing a blessing puts you as close to God as you can get. To learn to look with compassion on everything that is; to see past the terrifying demons outside to the bawling hearts within; to make the first move toward the other, however many times it takes to get close; to open your arms to what is instead of waiting until it is what it should be; to surrender the justice of your own cause for mercy; to surrender the priority of your own safety for love—this is to land at God's breast.[3]

Choosing Hope

The look of blessing transforms us by seeing the good that we may not yet recognize but that is truly there. A blessing will often begin with the word *may*, because it can imagine what might potentially be born in us out of the blessing. O'Donohue writes:

"The word *may* is the spring through which the Holy Spirit is invoked to surge into presence and effect. The Holy Spirit is the subtle presence and secret energy behind every blessing."[4]

Not long ago I received healing prayer for my fears around writing this book and telling my own stories. I wondered whether I had any stories and whether the ones I had were worthy to be told. Though I have tried to live a faithful life before God, I often feel more like the beggar asking to see, or the father who said, "Lord, I believe, help my unbelief!" than like someone who can offer wisdom to others. As we prayed, others prayed against the fear, but my own hearing was muffled by fear and doubt and disillusionment. Then my friend, a healing prayer teacher and practitioner, stopped the huddled prayer, looked me in the eye and asked me to stand up. The moment I stood up, I found my place with God and began to see blessing and possibility in my life and in the work I'd been given. When Heather looked me in the eye and told me to stand, I saw myself in the mirror of blessing instead of that of fear. It was the same clear-eyed look I received from the pastor of my youth as he sat at my hospital bedside.

God is not making things up for us or reinventing us from nothing when he blesses us. Rather, the light of Christ reveals the possibility of Christlikeness in each of us. O'Donohue describes blessing as a "robust and grounded presence; it issues from the confident depth of the hidden self, and its vision and force can transform what is deadlocked, numbed, and inevitable."[5]

Jesus began the Sermon on the Mount with the words "Blessed are the poor," "Blessed are those who mourn," "Blessed are the meek," even "Blessed are the persecuted." This is not a conditional blessing for a time when the grieving is over, or when there is money or even freedom. Right now, you are blessed; you are the light of the world. When a blessing is received and recognized, the fear-filled find courage, the despairing can feel hope, and the timid are able to name their desires. It changes even how we see difficult and painful events in our lives. As a twelve-year-old I would never have chosen to be in that hospital bed. Yet if I had not been in that bed, I would missed out on the blessing that transformed my life.

The look of blessing sees each person and all of life not out of the scarcity of what is not but in the enoughness of what is. O'Donohue laments that we all too often "continue to live like paupers though our inheritance of spirit is so vast. The quiet eternal that dwells in our souls is silent and subtle; in the activity of blessing it emerges to embrace and nurture us."[6] But this is God embracing not our heroic self but our ordinary human self.

Sometimes the search for abundance in our lives is evidence of our fear of scarcity. We hoard not just things and money but ideas and time and even vacation days while we pray for abundance. Is it because we are afraid that there will not be enough, never enough? Perhaps our root fear is that we ourselves are not enough. And such fear impoverishes our lives, despite the accumulation of stuff we may have gathered. When the Israelites cried out in hunger as they wandered in the wilderness, they were given manna to eat, enough for each day. But when they picked up more than they needed and kept it overnight, it became rotten and inedible. The things that we collect are equally unable to feed our hungers.

Jesus said, he came so that we "may have life, and have it abundantly" (John 10:10). This life to the full is given to us in Christ in the circumstances of our daily human lives. Everyone has enough time and money, enough personality and gifts, enough intelligence and intuition to be blessed with an abundant life. Abundance comes out of the recognition that in Christ there is enough.

Life in Christ is meant to return us to our creation in God's image and that first blessing from the Creator. The letter to the Ephesians calls the recovery of this inalienable identity "learning Christ" and being taught to "clothe yourselves with the new self, created according to the likeness of God in true righteousness and holiness" (Ephesians 4:20, 24). Salvation is itself the redemption of the image of God in us that has been obscured by sin, alienation and separation. It is not something we achieve but the grace of new life that is closer to the life the Creator intended from the beginning. In Colossians this redeemed return to humanity's original identity is described as the "new self . . . being renewed in knowledge according to the image of its creator" (Colossians 3:10). Through Christ and in Christ, the image of God is restored.

Perhaps the resistance to blessing that I often encounter in Christian communities is rooted in a fundamental distrust of the ability of even redeemed humanity to reflect the likeness of God. It's almost as if by practicing blessing we would disregard the power of sin and evil in ourselves and in the world. But blessing sees that sin and evil while insisting that the power of God's renewing Spirit is greater than the power of evil. Both creation and redemption turn our eyes to God's love, which begins before sin and which comes to us in Jesus Christ not merely to chastise us but to redeem sin's devastating consequences.

Any spiritual practice that is rooted in the unredeemed self begins with the intention of trying to win God's approval and ends in spiritual frustration. Guilt-ridden, it is based on human effort rather than God's love; its ending point is striving after a lost perfection, rather than healing forgiveness and gratefulness for a new life in Christ. Essentially, we find ourselves running after a holiness that is already God's gift to us in Jesus Christ.

Blessing, though, is a bit like the careful, painstakingly, even tedious work of preservationists or conservators who are restoring a painting or a sculpture or a cathedral to its original beauty. Their work is not creative, but it is recovering the original creator's intent in the color, the shape, even the material stuff that was used in its original creation. The conservator must both see the intention and pay attention to all the ways that use, disuse and abuse have tarnished its beauty, the color and shape and outline of what was meant to be. Blessing, too, seeks to recover what has been there all along but hidden by years of dirt, tarnished by the touch of others, wounded by neglect or even outright violence to the Creator's intention for us.

What is revealed to us by blessing is our God-created self in all our uniqueness. Seeing the diversity of self with all of the circumstances of family, gender, race, geography, culture, ability and disability that shaped us is at the heart of blessing. It honors individualism that can divide, but it deeply unites us in our common humanity. Blessing resists the homogeneity that would make each person just like another, and ignore the concrete singularity of our life's details and our life choices.

The look of blessing can be offered to colleagues at work, students in the classroom with us, the clerk at the grocery store or the people who commute with us by car or train or bus, because each person is made in the image of God. New Testament scholar N. T. Wright insists that bearing the image of God is our work in the world, calling it our unique calling.

> Bearing God's image is not just a fact, it is a vocation. It means being called to reflect into the world the creative and redemptive love of God. It means being made for relationship, for stewardship, for worship—or, to put it more vividly, for sex, gardening and God. Human beings know

in their bones that they are made for each other, made to look after and shape this world, made to worship the One in whose image they are made.[7]

God's grace extends blessing to those who think they are more than human because of pride or status or self-righteousness, as well as to those who see themselves as less than human because of guilt or shame or lack of status. The look of blessing requires us to look beyond our assumptions, cherished stereotypes and established preferences and see the look of love God offers to us and to those around us. But for that to happen, our hard looks toward ourselves and others need to soften so that we can see the goodness that is present already, so that they (and we) can reveal the presence of God. Softening our hard looks requires our cooperation but is ultimately the work of God's Spirit in us. The apostle Paul knew this when he blessed the Jesus followers in Rome with this blessing: "May the God of hope fill you with all joy and peace in believing, so that you may abound in hope by the power of the Holy Spirit" (Romans 15:13).

Living in Hope by Seeing Possibility

Listening to my life story. Most of us have a parent or grandparent, a sister or brother, an aunt or uncle, a teacher or counselor, a pastor or friend who has seen potential in us that we might have missed ourselves. Think about this person. How did his or her blessing make a difference in the way you understood yourself or in the life choices you have made?

Listening to the biblical story. Read 1 Peter 2:4-10. This letter was written to a disparate group of Jesus-followers who were shunned and sometimes persecuted by their neighbors. How does Peter bless them as he names them? How might this change their relationship to others or to themselves?

Listening to hope's continuing story. How do you understand the relationship between blessing and hope? How does your own identity in Christ encourage you to bless others?

Further Reading

O'Donohue, John. "To Retrieve the Lost Art of Blessing." In *To Bless the Space Between Us,* pp. 185-217. Garden City, NY: Doubleday, 2008.

Taylor, Barbara Brown. "The Practice of Pronouncing Blessings." In *An Altar in the World: A Geography of Faith,* pp. 193-209. New York: HarperOne, 2009.

9

Trusting Christ

Improvising a Life

Scared Scriptless is a long-running improvisational group performing together regularly in Anchorage, Alaska. On Wednesday evenings they offer two hours of supervised play for anyone who wants to join in on their games. Arriving for the first time one Wednesday at the "improv playground," as it is called, I'm terrified. I come in the door but then nearly turn around and get back into my car. I like to be prepared, but here I sense that I have to let go of any careful preparation. Worst still, I have to let go of personal control. Still, because I've talked about improvisation as an approach to my own vocation as a spiritual director, I sense a certain responsibility to follow through by actually participating in the activities I describe and encourage.

I'm greeted enthusiastically by the supervisor of this playground. He begins by insisting that there is no failure here; there are no mistakes, only opportunities. I remain dubious, especially as we begin to play the games where we pass a "whoosh" to someone and say a "whoa" to another, then a silly phrase that everyone mimics. I get my "whooshes" mixed up with my "whoas" and fail to either receive or pass at the rhythmic speed required. Nobody but me, however, seems bothered by these gaffes. The others just pick up the game where I dropped it and continue on.

In some games I need to pay close attention to the person next to me, while ignoring the others. In other games I need to watch everyone and be ready to act, or more properly interact, at a moment's notice with someone across from me in the circle. Some of the games prize memory, while others emphasize alertness; still others demand spontaneous physical movements that my body seems reluctant to do. And too often it seems I am required to do all of this simultaneously.

But in all of these games I learn to be attentive, ready at a moment's notice, not to overthink but to keep the idea of the game moving through the group as a whole. If I become self-conscious about my ability (or lack thereof) and don't focus on the action as a whole, I get lost in these fast-moving improvisations and cannot participate when the participating moment comes my way. I'm surprised at how much time we spend helping each other as a group to remember where we've been, because it is all incorporated into where we will be in a game.

If I am part of the game, I cannot simply be a spectator, even if I find myself a reluctant performer, even if I am more hesitant than spontaneous or anxious about participating rather than free to jump in. My mind tells me that I cannot do this, even while others urge me forward to try. So I often come into a game at the urging of someone else who physically pulls me in. When I become less self-conscious, I begin to notice how others play this game and the fun that they find in this playground. It seems that their concentration on the game itself rather than their self-consciousness is what turns this challenging interplay into a truly playful game.

After an hour of games we actually begin to play situations that resemble what I'd seen in public performances by Scared Scriptless. Then I find myself in group therapy, trying to guess the psychological malady that I have and that everyone else already in the mock group therapy session already knows about me. They give me clues and try to help me discover what my problem is. Later I find myself in a one-act, playing a disgruntled unicorn with a partner, also a unicorn. But our play is continuously interrupted by someone else's take on a one-act play with a totally different subject that we need to receive and incorporate into the situation.

Now I see that the games that seemed so silly are integral parts of the situations that unfold in improvisation itself. The games teach the skills that allow you to not only pay attention but be creatively present enough to enter the action and take it in a new direction. I realize that each week the same games are practiced over and over so that reactions can be more, rather than less, spontaneous and true.

After two hours of improvisational games and situations, I am completely exhausted but also exhilarated. How much easier it was to watch Scared Scriptless performances as part of the audience than to actually find myself scared scriptless! But I am also challenged to consider what it might be like to live my own life so at the ready to move in the direction that it might take me, rather than avoiding fear and failure at all costs.

What if I approached my own life as a story told one word at a time or responded to each eventuality with an open-ended "yes, and . . . ?" This might be an open-ended way for all of us to continue to live fully alive in Christ. What might it be like for us to receive the offer of life in Christ with a quizzical, hopeful

yes . . . *and?* Saying yes does not make us the author of our own
story, but it does make us a participant in the outcome. It allows
us to receive the past as a clue to what might come next, and the
future as a possibility. But most of all, it allows us to stand in the
present moment, accepting all that has been and all that is as
enough for all that will be.

Improvising a life in Christ is not about originality or clev-
erness, profundity or heroism. Instead it is about acting out of
practices and habits that are already who we are. It is about
being obvious and simple, clear-headed and attentive. The
practices and habits that already are a part of us give our improvising meaning and hope in Christ. Then what we perceive
as the givens or even the limitations of our own life can
become gifts.

> Experienced improvisers know that if they have attained a
> state of relaxed awareness, they can trust themselves to be
> obvious. . . . The practices and disciplines of Christian dis-
> cipleship aim to give the Christian this freedom—indeed,
> the skill—to be "obvious" in what might otherwise seem
> an anxious crisis. Those with relaxed awareness, who take
> right things for granted, are what the church calls saints.[1]

Practiced alone or together, relaxed awareness is not so different from abiding prayer that allows prayer to be more focused
on being with God than on doing, more about relationship than
about duty. In the weekly act of community worship we develop
habits of naming God's presence in community, listening for
God's Word, discernment in conflict and compassion in suffering. Congregational life can help us remember who is missing
and the virtue of love for those who are suffering physically,
emotionally or spiritually. That this is not always a reality in our
communities might be because we put ourselves in charge of the

action and the outcome rather than looking to God, who is still longing to create life with us.

I began the fall with big plans and high hopes for what I might accomplish. My proposed schedule was filled with teaching and writing commitments. Though this might be difficult, I felt no stranger to hard work. The good news was that I had the time that I needed and the uninterrupted schedule for working in the next three months, in the quiet of my Alaska home.

Then I received a telephone call from my husband, who told me that he would need open-heart surgery. Instead of decisions about what to put in the chapters of a book, there were decisions to be made about where to have surgery and who would do the surgery. Instead of meeting with online students, I began calling the insurance company and hospitals, doctors and cardiac care coordinators.

Peacefulness was replaced by anxiety about the surgery and any complications that might occur. Friends described this surgery as "routine but risky," which was surely meant to be comforting but became a further source of worry. What were the risks? What made this routine? And for whom was this routine? Surely not for my husband or for me.

A lawyer in our church community offered to make a health directive to be taken to the hospital, outlining Max's wishes (and mine) regarding any extraordinary care that might be needed in case of a life-threatening outcome. Again, her thoughtfulness and care only served to heighten my sense of emotional disequilibrium. A friend offered to come from California to provide postoperative care for my husband, while our oldest son insisted that he must be there for the surgery itself and the initial days of recovery.

I learned a whole new vocabulary about cardiac arterial bypass grafts (CABG) that I didn't know before. My life was filled now with visits to the cardiologist and the heart surgeon. During the surgery, an anesthesiologist and a perfusionist would place my husband on the heart/lung machine so that the surgeon could harvest veins for the bypass and use them to replace the occluded arteries. After the surgery I even met with an electro-cardio physiologist because of a concern over my husband's ir-regular heartbeats.

The bypass surgery did prove to be more routine than risky, and the medical directive was not needed. But in order for me to let go of my teaching and writing commitments, I needed to accept my husband's illness and my responsibilities for his care in light of the larger story of my love for him. And it was not just me who accepted in light of a larger story.

The women in a group that I lead, many of them with small children and busy lives, set aside the time to bring meals and provide other kinds of practical and emotional support to me and my husband. Just in time for the cold of winter, someone repaired the garage door opener, someone put away the summer furniture, and others raked the leaves.

Then there were prayers for healing that came from all over the state of Alaska, the United States and even the world as my own students in the Czech Republic, Japan and Laos joined their prayers with the prayers of the local community around us. My husband and I, who are often asked to pray for others, depended now on the prayers of our community. Once during this time someone came up to me to tell me outright, "You know that this community really loves you." I had no doubt about this, sur-rounded as I was by their prayerful, supportive presence.

Though some of this support was scheduled, none of it was planned. Our community, especially the faith community of

First Covenant Church, was simply improvising out of longtime habits of worship and compassionate care. In that sense my husband's health crisis was a gift to the community because it was a call to care, an opportunity to be the tangible presence of Jesus Christ. Some in my biological family thought my husband might want to go "outside," as we call the Lower 48 here in Alaska, where the procedure has been done even more times and where the "best" surgeons are to be found. But in the end, my husband knew that not only did he need the best surgeon to care for his body—he needed the body of Christ as well.

It is not hard for me to believe that your life has been upended as well by sickness, suffering and perhaps the death of someone you loved very dearly. Or the worst that you hoped to avoid now is with you in an unexpected diagnosis, a pink slip, a literal or figurative fall from where you thought you were standing securely. At those times our careful plans must be laid aside; our regular routines must be abandoned; our hard work and efforts seem to be futile; our masks of cheerfulness fail to hide our anxieties and fears for what might be ahead. Even happy events of shared love or the birth of a child can surprise us with their unexpected, surprisingly constant presence in our lives.

It is then that spiritual practices, now habits, remind us of God's love, welcome and blessing; they give us the graced faith to live in Christ one step at a time with our longings and vulnerabilities, they teach us how to pay attention to blessings even in difficult or stressed times. These habits of faith allow us to continue to live fully, receiving what must be received with God and the community of faith, until we realize that indeed God can be found in all things and we can truly encounter Christ's presence at every moment.

What if learning to live fully is less about making the right choice to please God or discerning God's will in the moment of crisis than about the development of habits of life and sight that help us to see where God's love is most needed or already at work? "For everything created by God is good, and nothing is to be rejected, provided it is received with thanksgiving" (1 Timothy 4:4).

Even sin is not a deterrent to experiencing that grace, as we see in the biblical story of Joseph. Despite his own brothers' efforts to kill him, Joseph recognizes that God has not been limited by their sins. God used their sins as a means of grace. As he reconciles with his brothers, he explains that he has been able to save their lives and the lives of others because of his position in Egypt. "God sent me before you to preserve for you a remnant on earth, and to keep alive for you many survivors. So it was not you who sent me here, but God" (Genesis 45:7-8). Human sin is overcome by God's providence. When Joseph is willing to respond not out of his abandonment but in light of the larger story of God's work, he brings not just food but healing to his family.

In the parable of the talents a master entrusts to his servants a talent, a sum of money. To one he gives five, to another two, and to another he gives one talent. Then he leaves on a journey. Upon his return, the servant who was given five talents reports that he put that money to work and made five more talents, while the servant who had two talents now brings two more talents to the master. The master commends them for their faithfulness and invites them to share his own happiness. But the person who got one talent says that he was frightened by the master's request, so he hid the one talent and now is returning it to the master.

His master is displeased that there is not at least interest accrued on the talent that he had left him. So he takes the one talent away and gives it to the servant who already has ten talents. Then the master says, "For to all those who have, more will be given, and they will have an abundance; but from those who have nothing, even what they have will be taken away" (Matthew 25:29).

Left with this startling ending to the story, one that might seem unfair, perhaps even cruel, we are left to wonder about the ethics of such a master. But the truth is that in the economy of spiritual faithfulness it is just so: the one who already has and is willing to spend it to get more *will* get more. And the one who out of fear hides the little that he has ends up with nothing at all. An analogy might be drawn with my husband's cardiac rehabilitation following his surgery. He might hesitate to go to the gym out of fear of pain, or fear of damaging something, but the more that he exercises, the more his health improves. Refusing to exercise would take away from him the good results of the surgery. The more he exercises, the healthier he will become. So too in the area of spiritual practices—the more we exercise and practice, the stronger our innate abilities to connect with God and others become.

Taking a Closer Look: Living the Rules of Improvisation

The first rule of improvisation is to agree and say yes. Improviser Tina Fey readily admits that we may not agree with everything that people say. Nevertheless, beginning with a yes means that we are starting with an open mind. We can at least say yes and see where this leads. "As an improviser, I always find it jarring when I meet someone in real life whose first answer is no. 'No we can't do that.' 'No, that's not in the budget.' 'No I will not hold your hand for a dollar.' What kind of a way is that to live?"[2]

The second rule of improvisation is to say not only yes but "yes, and." "By saying 'yes, and' you agree and add something of your own. . . . To me 'yes, and' means don't be afraid to contribute." Because, says Fey, "There are no mistakes, only opportunities."[3]

On the radio show *Fresh Air,* Tina Fey was being interviewed by Terry Gross when she turned the tables and asked Gross a question: "When you are working with a group improvising together, when do you come in?" Gross suggested maybe when you have something funny to say—a reasonable response, I thought. But Fey said this: "You only come in when you are needed."[4] You do not enter the story because you have something clever, witty or funny to say. It is always about carrying the story forward, even though there is no script.

Take a close look at your own life. In what area might God be asking you to "agree and say yes"? As you reflect on this situation, what would it be like to carry the story forward by saying "yes, and"? Where do you need to come in? Does the loving certainty of Christ's death and resurrection and his Spirit's continuing presence allow you to relax enough to let go of ways that are frozen in your life?

Christian discipleship is about keeping the story going. It may seem risky at times, but it does not need to be difficult. In Jesus Christ God has already brought the decisive elements into play, into the story. It is God's story that defines our story and not our story that explains God. Jesus wants to pull us into the story, but we cannot subvert its ultimate aim.

> The creative imagination is thus engaged in forming Christians to be the kind of people who have the courage to keep the story going, even when it looks dangerous or when it threatens to reveal uncomfortable parts of themselves. Belief in God's sovereignty affirms that the story *will* keep

going whether Christians are part of it or not. But the vocation of each Christian is to continue to be part of the story, to embody the story from the moment of baptism, regardless of the cost.[5]

Reformer Martin Luther suggested "brave sinning" (*pecca fortier*) not as a pathway toward reckless self-centeredness but actually to help graced disciples focus less on the self and more on living a joyful life of God-centerness. "God does not save people who are only pretended sinners. Be a sinner and sin bravely, but believe and rejoin Christ even more bravely, for he is victorious over sin, death and the world," advised Luther in a letter to his colleague Philipp Melanchthon in 1531.

Prayer Practice: Spiritual Direction

One of my favorite biblical pictures of loving companionship is Mary's visit to Elizabeth shortly after saying yes to the angel Gabriel to be the mother of Jesus, the Messiah. Mary comes quickly to her older friend, sensing that Elizabeth will help her to say "yes, and." The child within Elizabeth leaps for joy as she greets Mary at her door. "Elizabeth was filled with the Holy Spirit and exclaimed with a loud cry, 'Blessed are you among women, and blessed is the fruit of your womb. And why has this happened to me, that the mother of my Lord comes to me? For as soon as I heard the sound of your greeting, the child in my womb leaped for joy. And blessed is she who believed there would be a fulfillment of what was spoken to her by the Lord'" (Luke 1:41-45).

With this blessing from Elizabeth, Mary is now able to sing her Song of Praise, her Magnificat, receiving God's blessing. But she also has a new view of the larger story that holds her. While she is a participant, God is the author of the story. It is God who lifts up the lowly, scatters the proud, fills the hungry with good things and remembers Israel with mercy.

When I meet with people for spiritual direction, I want them, like Mary, to see how the life of Christ is with them in difficult times and joyful times. I want them to understand how God does not simply love them but takes delight in who they are, who they were created to be. I'm listening always for that life in Christ where my spirit meets with their spirit and we both sense the blessing of the Holy Spirit that Mary and Elizabeth felt. Sometimes it is only by grieving a loss, confessing a sin or letting go of an attachment to something that there will be space for the blessing to be revealed. That is also necessary work. But what I really long for is that those I see in spiritual direction would find a spacious sanctuary to see their true selves in Christ and enter fully into their own story.

The tools used by the spiritual director are deceptively simple—contemplative listening, a loving, welcoming spirit, wise discernment—employed within a relationship and with prayer. Sometimes I will pray with people directly, but I consider the whole time of spiritual direction to be prayer, because as we seek God together we are already on holy ground.

The spiritual director's role bears some resemblance to the role of the supervisor at the Scared Scriptless improvisational playground. The spiritual director does not so much direct as create a sanctuary where it is possible to listen both to God and to the desires and hopes of our own hearts. As a spiritual director, I try not to come in unless I'm needed. I know that even though someone may later recall something I said, it is fundamentally not about being original or profound or clever. Trying to be profound as a spiritual director is a trap, a seduction, just as being funny is a seduction for the improvising person in a comedy troupe. It takes the focus off the relationship between the person and God and directs it toward the spiritual director. Instead our time together is about offering the person's story back so that she or he can receive it back with meaning that is often beyond what I could have imagined. This is a necessary reminder that it is the Presence of God that is leading this narrative dance, and not me.

Choosing Hope

In the second half of my life I began reexamining my story. In earlier years, my story seemed to unfold so quickly that reflection was a luxury I could scarcely afford. Sometimes story lines seemed chosen for me, even when I thought I chose them. But the longer I looked, the more I was able to see individual chapters, each with its title and yet so clearly linked to what went before and what followed after. The table of contents began to emerge from within the whole of where I'd been. Still, the headings themselves proved to be superficial, unsatisfactory descriptors.

Then I decided to explore my life within the chapters, paragraph by paragraph, not to nail down each detail but to find the transitions—those word bridges that carried me over passages filled with confusion and uncertainty and back to a semblance of an outline. And there I found them, hidden in plain sight. The times I stood at the edge of a *for instance*, lived out of an *as a result* and *along with*—or simply, *later* or *first*. I found a casual *however*, a *therefore* and an *on the other hand* that took me to an entirely new place. They were all there alongside startling moments of *actually*, and *truly*, and *who knew*. I saw that I rarely understood that a transition was a bridge until I dared not only to speak it but also to walk over it to the other side. Looking at those bridges now, I understand that there was a necessary faithful discipleship in crossing them, and I see that the bridges themselves were constructed by God's grace.

As I continued to write down my life, I also saw moments when its flow seemed to stop at a dark dead-end place, and the way back, which I thought I had so clearly marked with my life's bread crumbs, was obliterated by the crows that traveled with me. Then it was only by trusting the transition into *but, God . . .* and all that is possible beyond what I could think or imagine that led me on and into the next chapter.

I smile, remembering well the naiveté that led me to believe I could actually "raise" children or "build" a marriage. Yet I see now how the children did grow up and the marriage was sustained over the years. Even my own vocation never remained static but changed and evolved in entirely unexpected ways.

Looking at my life thus far, I see that from the very beginning I was captured by something, and then by everything. I understand better how my mother and father, my sisters and brother, the village in Wisconsin where I was born, the church where I was baptized, set the tone and the mood for all that would follow. But what surprises me most is my life's definite shape. I see that the most consequential events in the narrative were usually unintended but seem now to be essential, not only to the flow but to the creativity embedded in my story as a whole.

I recognize that I should probably tie up loose ends, either by coming full circle to the place where I began as I find the overall meaning of the narrative or by issuing a personal mission statement. But accomplishing such wise profundity would require me to step outside my own narrative, losing the plot line and disrupting the flow. Now that I am again gripped by its themes and amazed by its particular shape, stepping out of the place where I am seems unwise, perhaps foolish and not very fun at all.

Instead I may just lift my head up occasionally and look around as I continue writing, hoping to get a truer perspective on where I am in the moment. For if I stop while the draft is still being written, the whole momentum of my narrative flow might slow down and then stop altogether. I decide to improvise as I go along, receiving all that is given each day and responding to it all with an open-ended *yes, and?* Maybe this is just the transitional bridge needed to carry my story line forward to its own grace-filled conclusion.

Look back on your life and you will find transitional bridges that led you to another place in your narrative. Maybe you were surprised as well with what you found on the other side.

Perhaps you reach the end of this book disappointed that there is no road map, no prescriptive path, no global positioning system for guidance to a destination. Instead there are only stories—my story, your story, the world's story. All of our stories are meant to be lived in the larger story of God's love in Jesus Christ. "The amorphous limpness so often associated with spirituality is given skeleton, sinews, definition, shape and energy by the term 'Jesus.'"[6] The glory of God is all of us fully alive in Christ with our own stories in their specific locations, with their particular circumstances. We are not "spectators to God; there is always a hand reaching out to pull us into the Trinitarian actions of holy creation, holy salvation, and holy community."[7] As in improvisation, the script is not set out for us in advance; instead we are free to act in our own unique way within life with God. When we allow ourselves to be pulled in, we "discover ourselves as unique participants—each of us one-of-a-kind—in the life of God."[8] Living with joyful abandon as those who are loved, who are given the gift of faith and hope as a reality rather than just wishful thinking, is the way we hold on to life with all of who we are and were created to be.

Theologian and writer Henri Nouwen was fascinated by the Flying Rodleighs, trapeze artists who perform for a German circus.

Rodleigh spoke with Nouwen about his flying and said that the real star of the flying trapeze was Joe, his catcher. "He has to be there for me with split-second precision and grab me out of the air as I come to him in the long jump. . . . When I fly to Joe, I have simply to stretch out my arms and hands and wait for him to catch me and pull me safely up. . . . A flyer must fly, and a catcher must catch and the flyer must trust, with outstretched arms, that his catcher will be there for him." Shortly before his death Nouwen wrote, "I want to live trusting the catcher."[9]

When we live fully in Christ, when we are all in with God, we can fly and trust the Catcher to be there for us.

Living in Hope by Improvising a Life in Christ

Listening to my life story. As you look back on your life, where do you see times when you risked carrying your own story forward beyond your understanding? When did you need to set aside your plans and improvise for the sake of others or for a larger purpose?

Listening to the biblical story. Read Luke 1:26-56. Mary is sometimes called the first disciple of Jesus. What is Mary's role as a follower of Jesus? What are the ways she needed to improvise after she said yes to the angel Gabriel, God's messenger?

Listening to hope's continuing story. What does it mean to be open and available and to come in when you're needed? How are you challenged to trust the larger story of God's work in your life and the life of the world if you see your role as improvisational?

Further Reading

Fey, Tina. "The Windy City, Full of Meat." In *Bossypants*, pp. 81-101. New York: Little, Brown, 2011.

Well, Samuel. "Drama as Improvisation." In *Improvisation: The Drama of Christian Ethics*, pp. 59-70. Grand Rapids: Brazos, 2004.

Acknowledgments

I am deeply grateful to

My friend Mandy Bankson for her constant love,
My reader Deb Steinkamp for believing in this book,
My First Covenant Church family for receiving and caring for me,
My writing group for inspiring me with their writing and their lives,
The Journey Center community for welcoming my creativity.

Appendix 1

Journeying Together Along
the Pathway of Love, Faith and Hope

Prepare

Read the chapter before meeting together, using a journal to note thoughts, feelings and questions that arise in you as you read.

Read

Listen to the opening story in the chapter again, reading it aloud if possible.

Remember

What story does this remind you of in your life? Allow each person to tell their story, letting the storyteller draw any understandings or insights they choose from it. An appropriate response to a heartfelt story is a simple "Thank you." The listeners let the storyteller speak without giving advice or suggestions, telling their own stories, or offering an ending to someone else's story.

Listen

What insights from the author's reflections seem to be especially important in choosing love, faith and hope?

Reflect

Take some personal time to reflect on the journal suggestion in the chapter, under the heading "Taking a Closer Look." Share your own insights from your journal or what it was like to reflect on this aspect of your own life with the members of your group or classmates.

Choose

Each chapter includes a section titled "Choosing Love" or "Choosing Faith" or "Choosing Hope"; it suggests some virtues that may come to fruition in us as a result of attending to love or faith or hope as our chosen way of life. How might these appear in your life together? Are there other types of spiritual growth that might happen in us?

Practice

Each chapter has a prayer practice to help you to live out love or faith or hope. Consider making the suggested practice in each chapter your own. Try to find space for God to give you the grace to grow in love, faith and hope. As you begin, pray for the grace that you desire—the specific aspect of faith or hope or love. Plan to check in with at least one other classmate or member of the group for encouragement and prayer during the time that you are apart from one another.

Appendix 2

Bibliography

Love

Au, Wilkie, and Noreen Cannon Au. *The Grateful Heart: Living the Christian Message*. New York: Paulist, 2013.

Benner, David. *Surrender to Love: Discovering the Heart of Christian Spirituality*. Downers Grove, IL: InterVarsity Press, 2003.

Calhoun, Adele Ahlberg. *Spiritual Disciplines Handbook: Practices That Transform Us*. Downers Grove, IL: InterVarsity Press, 2005.

Foster, Richard. *Prayer: Finding the Heart's True Home*. New York: HarperCollins, 1992.

Hauwerwas, Stanley, and Jean Vanier. *Living Gently in a Violent World: The Prophetic Witness of Weakness*. Downers Grove, IL: InterVarsity Press, 2008.

Jones, L. Gregory. *Embodying Forgiveness: A Theological Analysis*. Grand Rapids: Eerdmans, 1995.

————. "Forgiveness." In *Practicing Our Faith: A Way of Life for a Searching People*, edited by Dorothy C. Bass. San Francisco: Jossey-Bass, 1997.

Keating, Thomas. *Invitation to Love: The Way of Christian Contemplation*. New York: Continuum, 1994.

Manning, Brennan. *The Ragamuffin Gospel: Good News for the Bedraggled, Beat-Up and Burnt Out.* Portland, OR: Multnomah, 1990.

Nouwen, Henri J. M. *Return of the Prodigal: The Story of Homecoming.* New York: Continuum, 1999.

Nouwen, Henri J. M., Michael Christensen and Rebecca J. Laird. *Spiritual Formation: Following the Movements of the Spirit.* New York: HarperOne, 2010.

Reimer, Kevin. *Living L'Arche: Stories of Compassion, Love and Disability.* New York: Continuum, 2009.

Taylor, Barbara Brown. *An Altar in the World: A Geography of Faith.* New York: HarperCollins, 2009.

Tyler, Ann. *Saint Maybe.* New York: Ballantine Books, 1996.

Vanier, Jean. *Essential Writings.* Edited by Carolyn Whitney-Brown. Modern Spiritual Masters. Maryknoll, NY: Orbis, 2008.

Volf, Miroslav. *The End of Memory: Remembering Rightly in a Violent World.* Grand Rapids: Eerdmans, 2006.

———. *Free of Charge: Giving and Forgiving in a Culture Stripped of Grace.* Grand Rapids: Zondervan, 2005.

Wright, N. T. *The Lord and His Prayer.* Grand Rapids: Eerdmans, 1997.

Faith

Barry, William A. *A Friendship Like No Other: Experiencing God's Amazing Embrace.* Chicago: Loyola, 2008.

Barton, Ruth Haley. *Sacred Rhythms: Arranging Our Lives for Spiritual Transformation.* Downers Grove, IL: InterVarsity Press, 2006.

Benner, David. *Soulful Spirituality: Becoming Fully Alive and Deeply Human.* Grand Rapids: Brazos, 2011.

———. *Spirituality and the Awakened Self.* Grand Rapids: Brazos, 2012.

Brown, Brené. *Daring Greatly: How the Courage to Be Vulnerable Transforms the Way We Live, Love, Parent and Lead.* New York: Gotham Books, 2012.

Bourgeault, Cynthia. *Centering Prayer and Inner Awakening.* New York: Cowley, 2004.

Carlson, Kent, and Mike Lueken. *Renovation of the Church: What*

Happens When a Seeker Church Discovers Spiritual Formation. Downers Grove, IL: InterVarsity Press, 2011.

Casey, Michael. *Toward God: The Ancient Art of Western Prayer.* Rev. ed. Liguori, MO: Triumph Books, 1996.

Chittister, Joan. *Following the Path: The Search for a Life of Passion, Purpose and Joy.* New York: Image, 2012.

Eagleton, Terry. "The Nature of Evil." In *The Best Spiritual Writing 2013*, edited by Philip Zaleski. New York: Penguin, 2012.

Finley, James. "Experiencing the Presence of God." Interview by Gary Moon. *Conversations* 4, no. 2 (Fall 2006).

Halpin, Marlene. *Imagine That: Phantasy in Spiritual Direction.* Dubuque, IA: William C. Brown, 1986.

Issler, Klaus. *Living into the Life of Jesus: The Formation of Christian Character.* Downers Grove, IL: InterVarsity Press, 2012.

Kallistos of Diokleia. *The Power of the Name.* Collegeville, MN: St. John's Abbey, Cistercian Publications, 1986.

Kang, Joshua Choonmin. *Deep-Rooted in Christ: The Way of Transformation.* Downers Grove, IL: InterVarsity Press, 2007.

Mahan, Brian. *Forgetting Ourselves on Purpose: Vocation and the Ethics of Ambition.* San Francisco: Jossey-Bass, 2010.

McLaren, Brian. *Naked Spirituality: A Life with God in Ten Simple Words.* New York: HarperOne, 2012.

Palmer, Parker. *Hidden Wholeness: The Journey Toward An Undivided Life.* San Francisco: Jossey-Bass, 2004.

Pauw, Amy Plantinga. "Attending to the Gap Between Beliefs and Practices." In *Practicing Theology: Beliefs and Practices in Christian Life,* edited by Miroslav Volf and Dorothy Bass. Grand Rapids: Eerdmans, 2001.

Peterson, Eugene H. *Eat This Book: A Conversation in the Art of Spiritual Reading.* Grand Rapids: Eerdmans, 2006.

Silf, Margaret. *Inner Compass: An Invitation to Ignatian Spirituality.* Rev. ed. Chicago: Loyola, 1999.

Volf, Miroslav, and Dorothy Bass, eds. *Practicing Theology: Beliefs and Practices in Christian Life.* Grand Rapids: Eerdmans, 2001.

Willard, Dallas. *The Renovated Heart: Putting on the Character of Christ.* Colorado Springs: NavPress, 2002.

Wolterstorff, Nicholas. *Lament for a Son.* Grand Rapids: Eerdmans, 2005.

Wright, N. T. *The Challenge of Jesus: Rediscovering Who Jesus Was and Is.* Downers Grove, IL: InterVarsity Press, 1999.

Zaleski, Philip. *The Recollected Heart.* New York: HarperCollins, 1995.

Hope

Au, Wilkie. *The Enduring Heart: Spirituality for the Long Haul.* Mahwah, NJ: Paulist, 2000.

Duncan, David James. "Strategic Withdrawal." In *Best Spiritual Writing 2000,* edited by Philip Zaleski. New York: Penguin, 1999.

Fey, Tina. *Bossypants.* New York: Little, Brown, 2011.

Hiss, Tony. "Wonderlust." In *Best Spiritual Writing 2012,* edited by Philip Zaleski. New York: Penguin, 2011.

Muller, Wayne. *Sabbath: Restoring the Sacred Rhythm of Rest.* New York: Bantam Books, 1999.

Nouwen, Henri J. M., Michael J. Christiansen and Rebecca J. Laird. *Spiritual Direction: Wisdom for the Long Walk of Faith.* New York: HarperCollins, 2006.

O'Donohue, John. *To Bless the Space Between Us: A Book of Blessings.* New York: Doubleday, 2008.

Peterson, Eugene H. *Christ Plays in Ten Thousand Places: A Conversation in Spiritual Theology.* Grand Rapids: Eerdmans, 2005.

Rolheiser, Ronald. *The Shattered Lantern: Rediscovering a Felt Presence of God.* New York: Crossroads, 1995.

Steere, Douglas. *Prayer and Worship.* Richmond, IN: Friends United Press, 1988.

Wells, Samuel. *Improvisation: The Drama of Christian Ethics.* Grand Rapids: Brazos, 2004.

Notes

Introduction

[1]Anonymous, *The Cloud of Unknowing* (14th century).

[2]Daniel Taylor, *Creating a Spiritual Legacy: How to Share Your Stories, Values, and Wisdom* (Grand Rapids: Brazos, 2011), pp. 13-14.

1 Choosing Life

[1]Thomas Keating, *Invitation to Love: The Way of Christian Contemplation* (New York: Continuum, 1994), pp. 35-36.

[2]Sample breath prayers are from Adele Ahlberg Calhoun, *Spiritual Disciplines Handbook: Practices That Transform Us* (Downers Grove, IL: InterVarsity Press, 2005), p. 206.

[3]Richard Foster, *Prayer: Finding the Heart's True Home* (San Francisco: HarperCollins, 1992), p. 123.

[4]Ibid., p. 124.

[5]Henri J. M. Nouwen with Michael Christensen and Rebecca J. Laird, *Spiritual Formation: Following the Movements of the Spirit* (San Francisco: HarperOne, 2010), p. 77.

[6]Henri J. M. Nouwen, *The Return of the Prodigal Son: The Story of Homecoming* (New York: Continuum, 1999), p. 40.

[7]Ibid., p. 69.

[8]Ibid., p. 79.

[9]Ibid., p. 108.

[10]Ibid., pp. 109, 115.

2 Compassionate Hospitality

[1]David Benner, *Soulful Spirituality: Becoming Fully Alive and Deeply Human* (Grand Rapids: Brazos, 2011), pp. 120-21.

[2]Adapted from Kay Lindahl, *Practicing the Sacred Art of Listening: A Guide to Enrich Your Relationships and Kindle Your Spiritual Life—A Listening Center Workshop* (Woodstock, VT: Skylight, 2003), p. 32.

[3]Kevin Reimer, *Living L'Arche: Stories of Compassion, Love and Disability* (New York: Continuum, 2000), p. 59.

[4]Stanley Hauerwas and Jean Vanier, *Living Gently in a Violent World: The Prophetic Witness of Weakness* (Downers Grove, IL: InterVarsity Press, 2008), p. 26.

[5]Jean Vanier, *Essential Writings*, ed. Carolyn Whitney-Brown, Modern Spiritual Masters (Maryknoll, NY: Orbis Books, 2008), p. 96.

[6]Gregory Boyle, *Tattoos on the Heart: The Power of Boundless Compassion* (New York: Free Press, 2011), pp. 72, 77.

3 Forgiving as We Are Forgiven

[1]Anne Tyler, *Saint Maybe* (New York: Bantam Books, 1996), p. 109.

[2]Ibid., p. 315.

[3]L. Gregory Jones, "The Craft of Forgiveness," *Theology Today* 50:345-57.

[4]L. Gregory Jones, "Forgiveness," in *Practicing Our Faith*, ed. Dorothy Bass (San Francisco: Jossey-Bass, 1997), p. 137.

[5]Adapted and modified from Wilkie Au and Noreen Cannon Au, *The Grateful Heart* (Mahwah, NJ: Paulist, 2011), pp. 148-51.

[6]N. T. Wright, *The Lord and His Prayer* (Grand Rapids: Eerdmans, 1997), p. 2.

[7]Ibid.

[8]Miroslav Volf, *Free of Charge: Giving and Forgiving in a Culture Stripped of Grace* (Grand Rapids: Zondervan, 2005), p. 156.

[9]Miroslav Volf, *The End of Memory: Remembering Rightly* (Grand Rapids: Eerdmans, 2006), p. 27.

[10]Jones, "Forgiveness," p. 134.

[11]Christian Duquoc is quoted in ibid., p. 140.

4 Following Jesus

[1]Michael Casey, *Toward God: The Ancient Wisdom of Western Prayer*, rev. ed. (Liguori, MO: Triumph Books, 1996), p. 12.

[2]Ronald Rolheiser, *Holy Longing: The Search for a Christian Spirituality* (Garden City, NY: Image, 1999), p. 5.

[3]Ruth Haley Barton, *Sacred Rhythms: Arranging Our Lives for Spiritual Transformation* (Downers Grove, IL: InterVarsity Press, 2006), p. 32.

[4]Casey, *Toward God,* p. 15.

[5]Ann Ulanov and Barry Ulanov, *Primary Speech: A Psychology of Prayer* (Atlanta: John Knox, 1982), p. 20.

[6]Joan Chittister, *Following the Path* (Garden City, NY: Image, 2012), p. 45.

[7]Marlene Halpin, *Imagine That: Phantasy in Spiritual Direction* (Dubuque, IA: William C. Brown, 1986), pp. 23-25.

[8]Margaret Silf, *Inner Compass: Invitation to Ignatian Spirituality* (Chicago: Loyola, 1997), p. 153.

[9]Kent Carlson and Mike Lueken, *Renovation of the Church: What Happens When a Seeker Church Discovers Spiritual Formation* (Downers Grove, IL: InterVarsity Press), p. 35.

[10]Ibid., p. 121.

[11]David Benner, *Opening to God: Lectio Divina and Life as Prayer* (Downers Grove, IL: InterVarsity Press, 2010), p. 15.

[12]Doris Janzen Longacre, *More with Less Cookbook,* updated ed. (Harrisonburg, VA: Herald, 2011), p. 12.

[13]David Benner, *Desiring God's Will: Aligning Our Hearts with the Heart of God* (Downers Grove, IL: InterVarsity Press, 2005), p. 119.

5 Embracing Vulnerability

[1]Adapted from Cynthia Bourgeault, *Centering Prayer and Inner Awakening* (New York: Cowley, 2004), p. 112.

[2]David Benner, *Soulful Spirituality: Becoming Fully Alive and Deeply Human* (Grand Rapids: Brazos, 2011), p. 166.

[3]Ibid., p. 160.

[4]Nicholas Wolterstorff, *Lament for a Son* (Grand Rapids: Eerdmans, 1987), p. 69.

[5]Ibid., p. 70.

[6]Ibid., pp. 77-76.

[7]Ibid., p. 88.

[8]"Brené Brown: How Vulnerability Holds the Key to Emotional Intimacy," interview by Karen Bouris, *Spirituality and Health,* November-December 2012, http://spiritualityhealth.com/articles/bren%C3%A9-brown-how

-vulnerability-holds-key-emotional-intimacy.

[9]Henri J. M. Nouwen with Michael J. Christensen and Rebecca J. Laird, *Spiritual Formation: Following the Movements of the Spirit* (New York: HarperCollins, 2010), p. 43.

[10]Brené Brown, *Daring Greatly* (New York: Gotham Books, 2012), p. 117.

6 Living with Integrity

[1]Klaus Issler, *Living the Life of Jesus: The Formation of Christian Character* (Downers Grove, IL: InterVarsity Press, 2011), p. 36.

[2]Terry Eagleton, "The Nature of Evil," in *The Best Spiritual Writing 2013*, ed. Philip Zaleski (New York: Penguin, 2012), p. 17.

[3]Amy Pauw Plantinga, "Attending to the Gap Between Beliefs and Practices," in *Practicing Theology: Beliefs and Practices in Christian Life*, ed. Miroslav Volf and Dorothy Bass (Grand Rapids: Eerdmans, 2001), p. 48.

[4]Brian Mahan, *Forgetting Ourselves on Purpose: Vocation and the Ethics of Ambition* (San Francisco: Jossey-Bass, 2010), p. 184.

[5]Brian McLaren, *Naked Spirituality* (New York: HarperOne, 2012), p. 211.

[6]Kallistos of Diokleia, *The Power of the Name* (Collegeville, MN: St. John's Abbey, Cistercian Publications, 1986), pp. 8-9.

[7]James Finley, "Experiencing the Presence of God," interview by Gary Moon, *Conversations* 4, no. 2 (Fall 2006): 21.

[8]Philip Zaleski, *The Recollected Heart: A Guide to Making a Weekend Contemplative Retreat*, rev. ed. (Notre Dame, IN: Ave Maria, 2006), p. 78.

[9]Barbara Brown Taylor, *An Altar in the World: A Geography of Faith* (New York: HarperCollins, 2009), pp. 119-20.

[10]Eugene H. Peterson, *Eat This Book: A Conversation in the Art of Spiritual Reading* (Grand Rapids: Eerdmans, 2009), p. 28.

[11]Thomas Merton, quoted in Zaleski, *Recollected Heart*, p. 147.

[12]David Benner, *Spirituality and the Awakened Self* (Grand Rapids: Brazos, 2012), p. 123.

[13]George Herbert, *Heaven in Ordinary: George Herbert and His Writings*, ed. Philip Sheldrake (Norwich, England: Canterbury, 2009), p. 147.

7 Paying Attention

[1]Tony Hiss, "Wonderlust," in *Best Spiritual Writing 2012*, ed. Philip Zaleski (New York: Penguin, 2011), p. 79.

[2]Ibid., p. 84.

[3]Wayne Mueller, *Sabbath: Restoring the Rhythm of Rest* (New York: Bantam Books, 1999), p. 211.

[4]Douglas Steere, *Prayer and Worship* (Richmond, IN: Friends United Press, 1988), p. 11.

[5]David James Duncan, "Strategic Withdrawal," in *Best Spiritual Writing of 2000*, ed. Philip Zaleski (New York: Penguin, 1999), p. 56.

[6]Mueller, *Sabbath*, p. 176.

[7]Ronald Rolheiser, *The Shattered Lantern: Rediscovering a Felt Presence of God* (New York: Crossroad, 2005), p. 131.

8 Seeing Blessing

[1]John O'Donohue, *To Bless the Space Between Us: A Book of Blessings* (Garden City, NY: Doubleday, 2008), p. xv.

[2]Barbara Brown Taylor, *An Altar in the World: A Geography of Faith* (New York: HarperOne, 2010), p. 203.

[3]Ibid., p. 206.

[4]O'Donohue, *To Bless the Space Between Us*, p. xvi.

[5]Ibid., p. 207.

[6]Ibid., p. xv.

[7]N. T. Wright, *The Challenge of Jesus* (Downers Grove, IL: InterVarsity Press, 2011), p. 183.

9 Trusting Christ

[1]Samuel Wells, *Improvisation: The Drama of Theological Ethics* (Grand Rapids: Brazos, 2006), p. 65.

[2]Tina Fey, *Bossypants* (New York: Little, Brown, 2011), p. 84.

[3]Ibid., p. 85.

[4]Tina Fey, interview by Terry Gross, *Fresh Air*, National Public Radio, April 13, 2011.

[5]Wells, *Improvisation*, p. 96.

[6]Eugene H. Peterson, *Christ Plays in Ten Thousand Places: A Conversation in Spiritual Theology* (Grand Rapids: Eerdmans, 2005), p. 31.

[7]Ibid., p. 4.

[8]Ibid., p. 46.

[9]Henri J. M. Nouwen, Michael J. Christiansen and Rebecca Laird, *Spiritual Direction: Wisdom for the Long Walk of Faith* (New York: HarperCollins, 2006), p. 148.

formatio

TRADITION. EXPERIENCE.
TRANSFORMATION.

Formatio books from InterVarsity Press follow the rich tradition of the church in the journey of spiritual formation. These books are not merely about being informed, but about being transformed by Christ and conformed to his image. Formatio stands in InterVarsity Press's evangelical publishing tradition by integrating God's Word with spiritual practice and by prompting readers to move from inward change to outward witness. InterVarsity Press uses the chambered nautilus for Formatio, a symbol of spiritual formation because of its continual spiral journey outward as it moves from its center. We believe that each of us is made with a deep desire to be in God's presence. Formatio books help us to fulfill our deepest desires and to become our true selves in light of God's grace.

Also by Helen Cepero

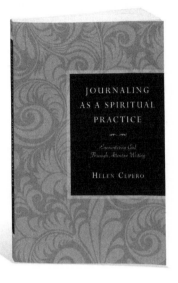

Journaling as a Spiritual Practice
978-0-8308-3519-5